# crying
## and
# laughing

## The Emotional Development
## of Infants and Toddlers

Donna S. Wittmer, PhD, and Deanna W. Clauson

Gryphon House
www.gryphonhouse.com

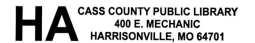

# Copyright

Library of Congress Control Number: 2020933683

# Bulk Purchase

Gryphon House books are available for special premiums and sales promotions as well as for fund-raising use. Special editions or book excerpts also can be created to specifications. For details, call 800.638.0928.

# Disclaimer

Gryphon House, Inc., cannot be held responsible for damage, mishap, or injury incurred during the use of or because of activities in this book. Appropriate and reasonable caution and adult supervision of children involved in activities and corresponding to the age and capability of each child involved are recommended at all times. Do not leave children unattended at any time. Observe safety and caution at all times.

This book is not intended to give legal or financial advice. All financial and legal opinions contained herein are from the personal research and experience of the author and are intended as educational material. Seek the advice of a qualified legal advisor or financial advisor before making legal or financial decisions.

# Table of Contents

# Acknowledgements

We would like to thank Stephanie Roselli, executive editor, for her support for our work, creative and technical insights that result in a beautiful book, and knowledge of the field of early childhood education that she constantly applies to improve the quality of books published by Gryphon House, Inc. We are grateful for her inspiring and personal whole-heart focus on respect for teachers of young children and relationship-based interactions and programs for infants and toddlers.

# Introduction

This book is for educational professionals who strive each day to facilitate and ensure infants' and toddlers' optimal emotional development and learning. It is for those professionals and families who want to learn more about emotional competence—the ability to understand, express, and manage emotions—that develops in the first three years of life. This book is for classroom teachers, family child-care providers, Head Start teachers and support staff, early intervention personnel, and parents and families who experience each day how important emotional competence is to the health and well-being of young children. We often refer to infant and toddler professionals as *teachers*, but know that we are talking about all professionals who strive each day to create opportunities for young children to flourish.

The book is organized around ten keys that early childhood professionals and families can use to support infant and toddler emotional development and learning. These keys will help you understand the power of emotions, the importance of emotional development and learning, the stages of emotional development, the many emotions that children ages birth to three express, and caring strategies that you can use to nurture very young children's emotional development and learning. We call these practical ideas *keys* because they open doors for you to help infants and toddlers develop and thrive emotionally. They open doors to the hearts and minds of young children.

When you put these keys to use, they are the foundation for helping children develop emotional competence. The approach outlined in this book is based on our observations in many child-care and learning programs, interviews with infant and toddler teachers, and many exciting research findings on emotional development. We offer knowledge and skills that will enable you to be compassionate infant and toddler professionals who provide the emotional nourishment that young children need. Within each key, we recognize the vital importance of partnering with families to enhance children's well-being. Each key also emphasizes the importance of teachers' culturally sensitive practices with children and in relationships with families.

It is you, the infant and toddler professionals, who know that a great start in life is vital for a child. You are the ones who listen to young children and understand their need to be seen and heard. You know that supporting emotional development in the early years creates a strong foundation that provides important life skills and resiliency. We hope this book enables and empowers you with the knowledge and tools you need to support emotionally healthy young children.

# Key ONE

Understand the Power of Emotions
and the Importance of Relationships

## In this chapter you will learn the following:

- The emotions that infants and toddlers experience

- The importance and power of emotions

- Emotional experiences that support children's learning about self and others

- The importance of caring relationships with adults for children's emotional health

- The influence of your feelings

Infants (birth to twelve months) and toddlers (twelve to thirty-six months) express many emotions with you throughout a day. You know from spending time with very young children that they do not show us how they feel just with their faces. They continually share their emotions through facial expressions, gestures, posture, body movements, words, and sounds (Keltner and Cordaro, 2015).

- An infant bursts out in gleeful laughter, his mouth open wide

- Another infant shows extreme distress or overwhelming fear through crying

- An infant whimpers and scrunches up his body

- A young toddler stomps his feet and furrows his eyebrows

- Another young toddler avoids looking at an angry adult and turns his body away

- An older toddler gleefully plays peekaboo with a peer

These behaviors are clues to whether these young children are feeling happy, sad, angry, or fearful. They may softly use words to tell you how they feel, or they may vigorously express themselves with their whole bodies and loud voices. As adults come to understand the meaning of these verbal and physical clues, they are often delighted and sometimes dismayed at the depth of infants' and toddlers' feelings and expressions.

Adults' interactions with infants and toddlers mostly happen on an emotional level. To meet young children's needs, teachers must relate to little ones' deepest emotions of fear, anger, sadness, grief, surprise, and happiness. It is essential for caring adults to use feelings and empathy to communicate with young children fully and effectively. Most importantly, children express their emotions within relationships. They use them to interact with others. They use their emotional expressions to be seen, heard, and loved (Lieberman, 2018). Infants and toddlers need to **feel** that their emotions matter to someone.

# The Emotions that Infants and Toddlers Experience

Each day you experience the facial expressions and body postures that tell you young children have many strong feelings. An infant sees your smiling face and feels happy. You know because he is smiling too. Another infant sees your fearful, worried face and feels fear. You know because of his facial expression. A toddler listens to the excited tone of your voice, looks where you are looking, and with eyes wide, looks surprised. When a beloved caregiver says goodbye, a young child may withdraw from others and feel sad. You know because of the child's face and slumping shoulders. When trying a new food, an infant's face may scrunch up in disgust. You may see a toddler express anger with furrowed brows and tense body if another toddler grabs a toy from him. These are a few of the many emotions that infants and toddlers are capable of expressing.

Carroll Izard was one of the early researchers who contributed to our understanding of young children's emotions. He studied the facial expressions that children use to tell us how they are feeling. He found that facial expressions for angry and sad, for example, occur in many different countries (Izard, 1971, 1977). Psychologist Paul Ekman (1999), who studied emotions, thought that six basic emotions (happiness, fear, surprise, sadness, disgust, and anger) occur in all cultures. He later added emotions such as contempt, pride, shame, embarrassment, and excitement to the list. Researcher Robert Plutchik (2002) concluded that there were eight basic emotions: joy, trust, fear, surprise, sadness, disgust, anger, and anticipation. He emphasized that each of these basic emotions can take many forms. For example, fear may become apprehension or terror; anger can become rage; joy may become serenity; and sadness can become grief.

As the research progressed, scientists identified twenty-seven distinct types of emotion (Cowen and Keltner, 2017). You have seen infants, toddlers, and family members express many of these emotions, including boredom, confusion, love, sympathy, shock, and amazement. Our concept of emotions continues to change as we gain a deeper understanding of the distinct types of emotions that humans experience. In this book, we highlight the emotions that infants and toddlers most commonly experience, based on what families, teachers, and researchers have observed in children ages birth to three years.

Each feeling has different dimensions and levels of intensity. Each feeling, however, is distinct.

Take a look at the following list of typical emotions that young children birth to three feel and express. How many have you recognized in the children you care for?

- Love, affection
- A sense of belonging, security
- Happiness, joy, glee, amusement, euphoria
- Satisfaction, calm, peace, serenity
- Surprise, curiosity, interest, amazement, excitement, anticipation

- Sadness, despair, grief
- Fear, anxiety, insecurity
- Anger, irritation, disgust, rage, hate, frustration
- Confidence, courage, pride
- Embarrassment, shame, guilt

Young children often express a sequence of feelings. They may start out feeling frustrated and then become angry. They may feel distressed and then become sad. No feelings are negative or positive. Each feeling is real, valid, and appropriate at times. Each feeling is important.

With each emotion children express, there are bodily changes within the child (Nummenmaa et al., 2014). When children are angry, the fight-or-flight hormone cortisol increases in their body. At high levels, cortisol can be damaging to the child's brain and general health (Bergland, 2015). Feeling happy results in a decrease in cortisol. When children are scared, their hearts beat faster and they breathe more quickly to increase their oxygen levels. These bodily changes are among the reasons adults want children to experience more feelings of love, happiness, security, and delight than they do anger, sadness, and fear.

# The Importance and Power of Emotions

It is hard to imagine a life without feelings. Emotions are at the core of our being and help each of us survive and thrive. How children experience emotions and how they express their feelings are major contributors to their healthy development. Young children's early experiences with emotions influence them throughout their lives.

Emotional health is necessary for young children to learn. When infants and toddlers are emotionally healthy, they express feelings in ways that create a sense of self-worth and loving, secure relationships with others. Infants and toddlers who feel unloved, rejected, fearful, angry, and sad much of the time may experience diminished emotional health. If experienced often, these emotions interfere with children's ability to focus, learn, and feel confident.

> "Early childhood education and care must create an equilibrium between academic achievements, such as literacy and numeracy, and attention to the 'emotional capital' of young children" (Murray and Palaiologou, 2018).

Children's emotions strongly influence us each moment we are with them. Throughout the day young children's feelings guide how we interact with them. Does an infant relax and smile in your arms? If so, you continue your responsive ways with him. If not, you adjust your behavior to help him feel calm, safe, and happy. Does a toddler express anger by striking out at a peer? If so, you try to help the upset toddler express his feelings with words and understand the other toddler's feelings. Adults sensitively interact with very young children based on their emotional expressions of happiness, sadness, wonder, anger, distress, and fear.

Infants and toddlers are also learning the power of others' emotions. As you can see in the following vignette, young children begin to change their behavior and feelings based on the emotional expressions of others.

Mattie, seven months old, tunes into the fearful face of her favorite caregiver and moves closer to her. Reading adults' facial expressions (called *social referencing*) tells Mattie whether a person or activity is safe or not (Mireault et al., 2014). Carl, a toddler, watches an adult angrily and loudly label a toy as bad. Afterward, Carl will not touch the toy while the adult is still looking at him (Repacholi et al., 2014).

The emotional expressions and connections that you share with infants and toddlers have a powerful effect on how they feel and what they do. We want young children to experience nurturing emotions and shared affirmative emotional moments with the adults who care about them. Only then will infants and toddlers gain the emotional knowledge they need to thrive.

# Supporting Children's Learning about Self and Others through Emotional Experiences

When you help children understand their own emotions, express their emotions in healthy ways, tune into others' emotions, and use emotions to develop caring relationships, you are helping them with one of the most important tasks of infancy. You are helping them learn the difference between self and others. Infants and toddlers are learning that they are people separate from others. They are learning that others may have feelings, thoughts, and experiences that are different from theirs.

One of the most important ways to help infants and toddlers learn about themselves and others is for you to share their emotions (Tremblay, Brun, and Nadel, 2005). An infant looks at you; a big smile graces his face, and you smile too. A toddler jumps for joy, and you laugh and enjoy the moment with him. During these important interactions, young children learn that they have feelings and others do too. You help infants and toddlers learn about peers' emotions when you point out how peers are feeling and encourage children to understand their friends' emotions.

# The Importance of Healthy, Caring Relationships with Adults and Peers

The affectionate connections that you create with infants and toddlers make a significant difference in how they learn to express and manage their feelings. Young children develop healthy relationships with you when they:

- feel that you read and understand their emotions and respond sensitively to them.

- feel safe to express all their feelings—even the ones that may be more challenging for adults to help them manage.

- can trust you to help them control their behavior and emotions.

- know that they can nestle into you or run to you when they are frightened, sad, or tired.

- can count on you to share their joy and sense of accomplishment.

- trust that you will help them negotiate challenging experiences with peers in ways that support and build their positive relationships with them.

Young children need to feel secure in your loving presence. They bloom emotionally when you are emotionally available to them.

Infants and toddlers thrive when observant and sensitive adults honor and respect their feelings. Researchers found that toddlers were more anxious and learned to hide their emotions if their parents punished them for their anger and frustration or minimized their emotions by saying, for example, "Stop crying. Don't be a baby" (Engle and McElwain, 2011). When children are upset, you can comfort them, talk with them, and help them work through their emotions.

Your relationships with infants and toddlers also grow when you find ways to respect their families' and cultures' unique ways of reacting to children's emotions, discussing emotions with their children, and expressing and modeling their own emotions (Raval and Walker, 2019).

Tina Marie, two years old, expressed her frustration by soft whimpering and quietly going to a teacher for help. After her teachers talked with the family about this, the mother and father both said that, while they value Tina Marie's expressing how she feels, they prefer she do it in quiet, less intense ways. With this information, Tina Marie's teachers learned to appreciate Tina Marie's soft voice that told them that she was often feeling as much as a child who cried loudly when frustrated.

Positive caring relationships with infants, toddlers, and families lead to the flourishing of children in your care and learning programs. These trusting relationships also enhance your enjoyment of children and your work as you share their laughter and soothe their crying.

# The Influence of Your Own Emotions

Because caring adults feel with young children, they are frequently trying to manage their own feelings, such as frustration and sadness, when they are with children. Working with infants, toddlers, and families can be extremely rewarding as well as tiring and frustrating. Your heart breaks for an infant who is ill. Feelings of frustration can bubble up inside you if a toddler continually hits other children.

Your emotions, too, result in bodily changes that may or may not be healthy. If you are frequently angry, frustrated, and discouraged, talk about your challenging feelings with coworkers and mentors. Reflect with them on why you may be feeling as you do and what you can do to feel and express emotions in healthy ways. Then you will be better able to model strong feelings for young children when you are with them.

# Summary

Use the following ideas from this chapter to support infants' and toddlers' emotional development.

- Understand the importance and power of emotions, and make positive emotional learning a priority in your program. Emotions help young children survive and thrive.

- Notice how children's emotions influence how we interact with them each moment.

- Observe and notice the emotions that infants and toddlers experience. It is important to notice each day how young children in your program understand and express emotions. You can then nourish and facilitate their emotional learning.

- Realize that emotional experiences support children's learning about self and others. One of the most important things that children learn in the first three years of life is to understand and express their own emotions. Young children also learn to understand and appreciate that others may experience and express emotions that are different from their own.

- Value the importance of healthy, caring relationships with adults. The emotional skills that you help children develop during the first three years influence their present and future success with learning and with adult and peer relationships.

- Recognize and reflect on the power of your feelings. How you express your feelings has a significant effect on infants' and toddlers' sense of well-being. You can manage your feelings and model the healthy expression of emotions each day in many ways.

# Key TWO

Know the Goals for
Children's Emotional Competence

- The many aspects of emotional competence— our goals for children

- How families' cultures influence their idea of emotional competence

Emotional competence includes young children's ability to express and manage strong emotions in healthy ways that support mental health and thriving relationships with others. It includes the ability to understand one's own and others' emotions and to treat others with compassion. Emotional competence includes the essential skills that children learn during their first three years to thrive in emotionally appropriate ways (Yates et al., 2008).

"The core features of emotional development include the ability to identify and understand one's own feelings, to accurately read and comprehend emotional states in others, to manage strong emotions and their expression in a constructive manner, to regulate one's own behavior, to develop empathy for others, and to establish and sustain relationships" (National Scientific Council on the Developing Child, 2004).

| Feature | Ability | Age: Infant | Age: Toddler |
| --- | --- | --- | --- |
| Emotional understanding and identification of their own emotions | • The ability to associate their own bodily reactions to names of feelings<br>• Recognition that they can experience multiple feelings | Not yet | Keisha, two-and-a-half years old, exclaims, "Me so mad!" to her mother who returned from a trip. |
| Emotional detection, understanding, and comprehension of others' emotions | The ability to notice, interpret, and appreciate how another adult or peer is feeling | Lotty, seven months old, stares at her teacher's fearful face. She quickly belly crawls to her teacher. | "You sad?" Axel, almost three years old, asks his teacher, who is looking sad. |
| Empathy and compassion for others' feelings and use of these feelings for the benefit of self and others | • The ability to feel empathy and compassion for others<br>• An ability to become involved in others' emotions<br>• The ability to engage in reciprocal (back-and-forth turn taking) and emotional sharing of feelings | Olivia, nine months old, looks concerned and reaches out to touch her crying friend. | Two-year-old Damont runs to get a sticker for Karlene, who is crying. He tilts his head to the side and looks sad as he offers Karlene the sticker. |
| Emotional expression | • The ability to demonstrate feelings through gestures, sounds, body movements, and language<br>• The ability to learn a language(s) to express emotions | Bodhi, three months old, scrunches up his face and then lets out a yowl.<br><br>One-year-old Ada leans her head to the side and smiles her biggest smile. | Nigel, twenty-two months old, bounces up and down with excitement. |
| Use of emotions for relationship building, a recognition that one's emotional expressions and behavior affect others | The ability to use emotional expressions to relate in healthy ways to others | Amrita, nine months old, smiles at her teacher. Her teacher smiles back at her. Later, Amrita smiles again and looks to her teacher for her returning smile. | Eitan, twenty-seven months old, scrambles closer to his friend, smiles widely, and asks, "Outside?" Eitan's friend smiles and takes Eitan's hand. |

| Feature | Ability | Age: Infant | Age: Toddler |
|---|---|---|---|
| Use of emotions to get needs met | The ability to use emotional expressions to get needs met | With furrowed brows, Mattie, five months old, looks up at her teacher. Her teacher responds, "Are you hungry, Mattie?" | Shannon takes Luis's toy out of his hand and runs away. Luis collapses on the floor crying. |
| Emotion regulation and coregulation | The ability to manage and express emotions in healthy ways (often with adult help) | Autumn, five months old, sucks her thumb and becomes calm. | Sid, fifteen months old, cries when his father says goodbye in the morning but then holds his stuffed bunny tightly while he snuggles in the arms of his favorite teacher. |
| Emotional self-efficacy | The child's belief in her ability to manage emotions in productive and healthy ways | Not yet | Hasan, twenty-eight months old, holds his hands behind his back to avoid hitting anyone when he is angry. Instead, his face expresses his anger to a peer. |
| Emotional resilience | The ability to manage feelings or recover after difficult, disappointing, or challenging emotional experiences | Camilla, five months old, stops crying when her teacher cradles her in his arms. | Nicolás, almost three years old, is sad because his friend has moved away. He plaintively says to his teacher, "I sad Felipe move. I no find him." |
| Emotional refueling | The ability to gain emotional energy to use for tasks and learning from adults whom the young child trusts | Henry, one year old, toddles over to his teacher and plops into her lap. He nestles in for about two minutes. His teacher talks softly to him, and soon he is off playing again. | Mariana, thirty months old, sits on the floor by her teacher. She stays there for half an hour and then runs off to play. |

| Feature | Ability | Age: Infant | Age: Toddler |
|---|---|---|---|
| Emotional intelligence | • The ability to understand one's own and others' feelings, to express feelings, and to use emotions in ways that benefit oneself and others<br>• Involves the skill of realizing that one does not always need to express behaviorally how one is feeling | Six-month-old Sofia's teacher observes the beginnings of emotional intelligence in Sofia. She expresses a range of emotions as she engages with others. She responds differently to fearful and happy emotions, for example. | Thomas, almost three years old, wants to hit Marco, who took his toy. "I tell you, I angry," Thomas declares, instead of striking Marco. |

Let us examine closely each of these important emotional strengths that we want to help infants and toddlers develop.

# Emotional Understanding and Identification of Their Own Feelings

Emotional competence includes children's emotional understanding and identification of their own feelings (Fernández-Sánchez et al., 2014). Infants and toddlers slowly begin to develop an understanding of their own emotions. Toddlers begin to identify and name their own emotions. Instead of falling apart on the floor in emotional frustration, toddlers often can use their words to exclaim how they are feeling, as Caryn, Gabriel, and Sebastián demonstrate:

> Two-year-old Caryn, with head in her hands, cries with feeling, "Me sad. Me crying." Gabriel, two, proclaims with a smile and a wet kiss, "I wuv you." Sebastián, almost three, yells loudly so all can hear, "I miss Papa!"

"The goal shouldn't be to shame or punish [for expressing emotions] but to provide the child with clear labels that **describe** her emotions and the **causes** for those emotions" (Ravindran, McElwain, Berry, and Kramer, 2017). (Emphasis added)

Young children also begin to develop an understanding of why they feel the way they do. Help young children learn both the labels for their feelings and the causes of their feelings. Talk to them about their emotions and why they may be feeling the way they do. For example, a teacher can say to a toddler, "You seem sad. You feel sad when someone takes your toy."

# Emotional Detection, Understanding, and Comprehension of Others' Emotions

"You sad?" Martin thoughtfully asks his mother as he pats her on her back—as she has done for him many times.

Throughout the first three years, young children learn to read other people's emotions. This is called emotional detection, understanding, and comprehension. Infants are sensitive to emotions—especially fear and anger (Peltola et al., 2015). Toddlers can even distinguish the differences between real and fake emotional expressions. One study found that eighteen-month-olds can detect whether an adult is faking an emotion or displaying an emotion that does not fit with the circumstance. For example, in the research of Chiarella and Poulin-Dubois (2015), if an adult looked pained when she should have looked happy because another researcher gave her something nice, the toddler was not likely to show empathy for that adult. However, if an

Crying and Laughing: The Emotional Development of Infants and Toddlers

adult looked pained after pretending to hit a thumb with a hammer while trying to hammer a peg, then eighteen-month-olds were likely to show empathy. Toddlers, then, were more likely to show empathy if they thought that the adult was really in pain and not faking pain.

Emotional comprehension is important because toddlers who begin to understand the feelings of others are more likely to be *prosocial*—kind, helpful, and empathic (Brownell et al., 2013). First, children learn to detect others' emotions. They perceive the feelings of others and learn how to respond. Their understanding of others' emotions influences whether they react or ignore another's distress (Ensor and Hughes, 2005).

Then, they are more likely to feel empathy and compassion for others. Belacchi and Farina (2012) found in their research that when preschool children understand others' emotions, they are more likely to be perceived by teachers as empathic, adaptable, and social. Emotional-detection skills are important for young children in developing social relationships. Understanding the causes of others' emotions develops, for example, when teachers explain why another child might be crying (Ravindran et al., 2017).

# Empathy and Compassion for Others

*Empathy* is the ability to understand and share the feelings of another. *Compassion* is the awareness of others' distress and the desire to do something about it. Only when young children feel empathy and compassion for others will they be able to develop mutually satisfying relationships with others.

*Affective empathy* involves feeling what another person is feeling. *Cognitive empathy* involves understanding another's feelings but not necessarily feeling what the other person is feeling (Belacchi and Farina, 2012). With both types of empathy, adults want children to genuinely care about others' emotions and respond with appropriate emotions.

Children who feel compassion for others feel motivated to relieve the suffering of others. We want infants and toddlers to learn what to do with their affective and cognitive empathy. During the first three years of life, you can support young children in thinking of wonderful ideas about how to help, comfort, soothe, and behave in ways that support others' well-being.

Jacob, eighteen months old, started crying when his mother said goodbye in the morning. Nineteen-month-old Sam stood and watched with a concerned look on his face. His teacher, Marcella, leaned down and asked Sam, "Would you like to take Jacob his favorite train? It might make Jacob feel better." Sam ran across the room, grabbed the train, and ran to Jacob. As he handed it to him, Jacob stopped crying.

# Emotional Expression

Infants and toddlers learn the body movements, facial expressions, sounds, gestures, and words to communicate their feelings, which is called *emotional expression*. Adults "read" the faces of young children as clear windows into their feelings. Developmentally, crying and fussing appear first, followed by the smile that lights up parents' and teachers' lives. Infants squirm and turn away or nestle into our bodies to tell us how they are feeling. Angry expressions occur early in infancy and express to sensitive adults an infant's discontentment and frustration. Sad or pouting faces occur in infants younger than six months of age (Sullivan and Carmody, 2018). Toddlers are just learning to use words and still mostly express their feelings with body movements, gestures, and sounds. They also begin to exclaim, "No!" to communicate their disgust for a new food or not wanting to wear a bib. Two-year-old children can often express their feelings quite clearly, as Veda demonstrates:

> With hands on her hips, Veda expressed her feelings about a separation from her father when he said goodbye at the door of the center. "Me no like dat," she declared.

The ability of young children to express their feelings in healthy ways with words influences how they feel. Toddlers with better language skills appear less angry at four years of age than their peers who are more challenged with language (Roben et al., 2013). This may be because expressing their feelings with words helps them to feel less frustrated or angry than children who have difficulty expressing their needs with language.

# Using Emotions for Relationship Building

One aspect of emotional expression is emotional use (Wilutzky, 2015). Children recognize that their expressions and behaviors affect others. Adults see children use their emotional expressions for many social purposes. For example, an infant's smile conveys a positive emotion (Campos et al., 2015) that adults interpret as a desire to make a social connection. The words, "Go 'way," uttered angrily by a toddler may achieve her goal of clearing a space for her to play. The words, "I wuv you. You the best baby sister," spoken warmly and with feeling by an almost three-year-old to her one-year-old sibling achieves the older sister's goal of making her sister smile. Young children learn to use their emotional expressions to develop and maintain relationships.

When infants smile and toddlers engage you with their eyes, these children are using their emotions to build relationships with you. It has been found that children at twenty-four months old use more looks of sadness with their mothers than with others. The researchers who noticed this behavior concluded that toddlers use their sad emotional expressions to gain support from their mothers (Buss and Kiel, 2004).

# Using Emotions to Get Needs Met

Carmen, a two-year-old, shows an angry face to her peer who just grabbed her toy. Carmen has the goal of getting her toy back.

Infants and toddlers use their emotional expressions to get their needs met. Often, infants and toddlers do not consciously have a goal; they are expressing openly and loudly how they feel. Soon, however, as adults and peers respond to children's emotional expressions, children learn to use them to get their needs met. An infant's eyes begin to water, and her face tells you she is about to cry. You then try to figure out why she feels sad or scared. Consequently, the infant learns that her facial expressions have meaning and will elicit a response from an adult. A toddler looks fearful. You look at where she is gazing and realize a dog outside the play-yard fence is frightening to her. When you respond, you help the toddler understand that fearful emotional expressions often lead to adult support. Soon a toddler can say, "Help," when she is frustrated. She has learned that emotions coupled with words will get her needs met.

# Emotion Regulation and Emotion Coregulation

Throughout their early years, with our caring support, young children gradually learn emotion regulation—the ability to express and control their emotions and their behavior in healthy ways. With young children, self-regulation is really coregulation: They need adults to support and teach healthy expression of feelings.

Using coregulation strategies with infants and toddlers helps them learn to control their strong emotions as you partner emotionally with them. Coregulation strategies include the following:

- Comforting upset infants by rocking them, talking gently with them, and holding them as you walk around to help them feel how to become calm

- Soothing infants and toddlers who are hurt or upset with your voice and hugs (if they want them) to help them feel that they can trust you to help them feel good again

- Assuring, through your words and behavior, that older infants and toddlers can come to you when they are feeling strong emotions to help them feel in control of their feelings again

- Encouraging toddlers to use sign language or words to express their feelings to others to help them learn to manage their emotions with language

- Encouraging toddlers who are upset to ask a peer to go to a cozy corner with them, to give them a strategy to relate to their peers when upset

- Asking older toddlers, "What can you do when you feel angry [sad, disappointed, frustrated]?" to encourage them to problem-solve ideas that work for them

Young children need you to coregulate their emotions.

Some young children have learned strategies that work for them. For example, some suck their thumbs when they are upset, tired, or emotionally exhausted. Other children settle in near you. Others may go to a cozy corner and grasp a soft blanket. They are demonstrating emotion regulation. You support their emotion regulation by creating a safe environment with you and the materials in the room. You support them by being there when they need you.

Infants and toddlers are beginning to learn to control emotional intensity. At first, an infant might cry loudly when she is hungry, and a toddler might scream when she is in pain. Gradually, children will begin to control or regulate how intensely they express emotions. For example, exuberant children are often fun to be with. They are playful and typically happy. If they're too exuberant, however, they might overwhelm their peers by bouncing around and cheerfully taking their toys. Slowly, many toddlers begin to learn to control their exuberance, so that peers will continue playing with them. Notice how, in the following example, Carla learns to manage her overwhelming positive feelings for Shawna.

> Carla, a child who expresses her feelings openly and loudly, wanted to play with Shawna. First, overwhelmed with her desire to play with Shawna, Carla tightly wrapped her arms around her friend in an intense hug. As Shawna protested, Carla stopped hugging and instead moved in front of her and smiled. Carla was able to control and change how she expressed her strong feelings so that Shawna would not run away.

Emotion regulation is a challenging task for young children. When Renee, a toddler, quickly grabbed Samir's toy, Samir's first feeling may have been anger. He may have wanted to hit Renee. However, with the help of caring and responsive adults, Samir will learn that rather than hitting or biting, he can say, "No take my toy," or "I need my toy." Being able to regulate emotional intensity predicts a young child's success with peers (Dollar et al., 2017).

# Emotional Self-Efficacy

As toddlers develop, many become confident and successful in their ability to express and manage their emotions. A toddler is unlikely to say, "Look! I'm telling my peer that I need my toy when she takes it from me."

However, you will observe many toddlers negotiating or taking turns with peers or telling peers how they feel when there is a conflict over space or toys. They are beginning to understand that they have the skills to manage strong emotions and to solve problems.

# Emotional Resilience

*Emotional resilience* refers to young children's ability to adapt to challenges that they experience. Adults should not expect young children to adapt to traumatic situations, such as neglect and abuse, without extensive help from supportive adults. We can hope, however, that young children will be able to handle disappointment and typical childhood stresses such as changes in schedules. During the first three years, children are just learning how to be resilient with the caring support of emotionally sensitive adults in their lives.

When you hold and soothe a child who is crying or sing songs with toddlers while they wait for a delayed lunch, you are helping them develop emotional resilience. You might help find a bandage for a child's scrape or take the time to explain in simple words to a child why a routine must change. As you respond, you acknowledge that you know they are feeling sad or frustrated. Empathizing with a child, helping to name her feelings, and then offering solutions helps her learn how to work through challenging emotions.

# Emotional Refueling

Older infants and toddlers learn to emotionally refuel with adults they trust (Mahler et al., 1973). They will go to their caregiver and nestle in—often for just a moment, but sometimes all day—as they gain emotional strength to continue their play. Observant teachers provide what each unique child needs to help that child gain or regain emotional energy—a warm look, a calming pat, a soothing hug, a soft shoulder to nestle into, or a welcoming spot near them.

We want young children to know how to refuel their emotional strength with those they trust. We want them to know that they can come to us when they are feeling sad, angry, or frustrated. They need to know that they are not alone in struggling with their emotions.

# Emotional Intelligence

Even as adults, understanding and expressing our own feelings can be challenging. *Emotional intelligence* means we develop an awareness of our own emotions, use our emotions to guide our behavior, and tune in to emotional signs from others. We use emotions to navigate our environment successfully. We can demonstrate this emotional intelligence to young children to help them develop their own skills. Young children's emotional intelligence involves the following skills:

- Beginning to understand the meaning of others' emotional expressions
- Recognizing and labeling their own feelings
- Expressing feelings in healthy ways with facial expressions, body movements, and language
- Using feelings in ways that benefit themselves and others

Many infants begin to demonstrate emotional intelligence. During their first year, they start to recognize the facial expressions of their favorite adults and respond in ways that benefit themselves. For example, a seven-month-old infant may look to your face to see whether a stranger is safe or not.

Many infants who receive prompt responses to their efforts to communicate their feelings and needs are learning what to expect from others when they smile, cry, shriek, or furrow their brows. Infants who expect smiles when they interact with their favorite adults will become upset when they smile and the adult doesn't smile back but instead has a face with a blank expression (Mcquaid et al., 2009).

Young toddlers tune in to adults' and peers' faces. For example, a toddler avoids touching a toy after an adult has expressed displeasure with it and is looking at the child (Repacholi et al., 2014). However, when the adult turns her back or hides her eyes, the toddler knows that the adult can't see her, and she then plays with the toy (Repacholi et al., 2008). These toddlers are demonstrating their understanding of the meaning of another's expression of emotion.

Many older toddlers become adept at recognizing, expressing, and labeling their own emotions. You may hear, "I tired," "Me angry," "I sad and mad." Young children use emotional expressions, such as smiling and frowning, to get their needs met or to relate to others. Older toddlers also may begin to learn that they do not always need to express behaviorally how they are feeling. For example, a two-year-old who feels angry may be able to control her desire to express that anger with a hit or a bite. This happens if a caring adult has helped her learn strategies for managing her anger in other ways.

# Emotional Competence: The Influence of Culture and Diversity

It is important to remember that how children demonstrate these essential skills may differ based on a child's culture. Culture includes the language, religion, social habits, beliefs, values, and ways of doing things that are used or considered acceptable by a group of people. Culture influences all aspects of infants' and toddlers' behavior. Young children are constantly learning about the value of emotions and how they should express them, based on their culture and experiences. Cultural experiences influence whether children feel as if they can or should share emotions and how they can or should manage, express, and control emotions (Ford and Mauss, 2015).

> Mac, two-and-a-half, runs to her teacher and says loudly, "Help! I feel angry." She is trying to tell her teacher very clearly that she is upset because Tamika has knocked down her block building. Mac uses words and tone of voice to express her anger. In contrast, instead of reacting loudly about how he is feeling when a peer knocks down his block building, Damion moves in close to the teacher, takes the teacher's face gently in his hands, and asks for help. He looks angry but doesn't express his anger in words or tone of voice. Damion is expressing his feelings through facial expressions and body movements.

Young children learn in their families and child-care and learning environments when, how, and where it is appropriate to talk about emotions. Families' use of culturally diverse emotional socialization strategies influences children's understanding and expression of emotions. According to Raval and Walker (2019), these strategies differ among cultures in three ways:

1. Parental reactions to children's emotions: For example, one parent may notice and show compassion for a child who has a sad face. Another parent may notice but ignore or diminish that child's feelings.

2. Parental discussion of emotions with children: For example, one parent may talk about different emotions with her child. Another parent may rarely identify the names of emotions.

3. Parental expression and modeling of their own emotions: For example, one parent may openly express and name her own emotions. Another parent may rarely express her feelings and think that it is important to hide feelings such as sadness.

Emotional socialization occurs early. For example, infants from Chile and the United States differ in how intensely they express their emotions at around one year of age. American infants express both their pleasure and discomfort more loudly than infants from Chile (Muzard et al., 2017). In some cultures, children may feel more comfortable carefully controlling their emotions. In other cultures, children may experience a sense of well-being when they freely express their emotions of happiness, sadness, anger, fear, and surprise (Ford and Mauss, 2015). Whether a behavior is considered emotionally competent, especially in expressing and managing their emotions, may differ based on the child's family and culture. Your culture, too, may influence how you react to children's and teammates' emotions, discuss children's emotions, and express emotions.

With cultural knowledge and thoughtful reflection, you can carefully evaluate your expectations for each child. While *you* may value all young children expressing their emotions freely with everyone, if a child's culture emphasizes that children should only express their personal feelings with those whom the family trusts, you

Crying and Laughing: The Emotional Development of Infants and Toddlers

will understand. When you understand a family's cultural expectations for their child's emotional competence and each child's unique way of expressing and managing her emotions, you will give each family and child the gift of respect and acceptance.

# Summary

Use the following ideas from this chapter to support infants' and toddlers' emotional competence.

- Reflect on the goals of programs and teachers to support healthy emotional development and competence that is individually and culturally appropriate.

- Observe and facilitate the development of many aspects of emotional competence.

- Reflect with your team and talk with families about the knowledge and skills that you and they want infants and toddlers to develop in the first three years.

- Discuss ideas with coworkers for strategies to develop each aspect of emotional competence.

- Observe how children's cultures influence how they express emotional competence. Reflect on why some children may express their emotions openly and freely (and sometimes loudly). Reflect on why some children may carefully control their emotional expression.

- Interview families to discover how they define emotional competence in their family and culture. Ask them what emotional knowledge and skills they would most like their children to develop in the first three years of life.

- Reflect with team members how your culture influences your understanding and expression of emotions. Think about which children's emotions bring you joy and which ones challenge you emotionally.

# Key

# THREE

Understand Brain Development and the
Importance of Emotional Competence

This chapter emphasizes the importance of optimal emotional development in young children's ability to survive and thrive. It includes many reasons why teachers and programs who work with infants and toddlers need to prioritize the emotional competence of young children.

## In this chapter you will learn the following:

- The importance of appreciating infants' and toddlers' emotional capital

- How the emotional brain develops, including how emotional development is built into the architecture of the brain

- How emotional competence is the key to children's success in life and in school

- The importance of emotion regulation for young children's success with relationships and academics

- Strategies to use to support children's optimal emotional brain development

- The experiences that limit children's emotional brain development

Emotional development is the absolute bedrock upon which learning can occur. When you as a birth-to-three professional focus on children's emotional development, you are creating a vital foundation that children will build on throughout their lives.

# Appreciating Young Children's Emotional Capital

Infants and toddlers are remarkably skilled at recognizing, interpreting, and expressing feelings to navigate their sometimes joyous and sometimes challenging worlds. Andi Salamon et al. (2017) explain that young children have emotional capital or capacities that they use to relate to others. From the moment they are born, babies have the brain structures to engage with others, express emotions, and learn about emotions in their interactions with their special adults, siblings, and peers.

Infants and toddlers are capable of learning that their expressions of emotions get results in interactions with others. At birth, their emotional ability includes making sounds that are endearing to the adults who care for them. They learn that a smile engages a loved adult. Gradually, as they become toddlers, they learn that their slumped shoulders and bowed heads call forth the sympathy of their favorite adults.

Infants and toddlers use both positive and negative emotional information from others to guide their social behavior (Leventon and Bauer, 2013). Infants begin to "read" others' faces for signs of joy, sadness, anger, and fear (Fernández-Sánchez et al., 2014). Infants at five months of age can hear a voice that expresses emotion (for example, anger) and then look to the picture of a face that is expressing that emotion (Vallian-Molina et al., 2013).

You can admire and appreciate the marvelous abilities of young children to engage with others, learn from others, and solve problems using their wealth of emotions. As you will see in the next section, however, the optimal development of the emotional brain after birth depends on supportive and nourishing interactions with responsive adults, siblings, and peers. In children's first three years of life, you help young children develop the brain structures that predict how they will feel and relate to others, both now and when they are older.

# The Emotional Brain

The emotional brain consists of the parts, structures, and neural pathways of the brain that are tied to how we process and feel emotion. The limbic system is responsible for processing emotions. Part of the limbic system, the amygdala assesses the importance of emotional information. The hypothalamus regulates or manages how we respond to emotions. Many of these same places in our brain are tied to learning, sensory stimulation, impulse control, and the ability to distinguish between what is good and bad. Emotions are part of children's complex neural systems that help them survive (LeDoux and Brown, 2017). Development of the emotional brain, then, is not just about learning to process and regulate emotions but has far-reaching effects on many aspects of a child's well-being and future self.

The first three years are especially important for children's emotional brain development. During the first year of life, adult-like brain connections for understanding, expressing, and managing emotions emerge. During the second year of life, the growth of these brain circuits predicts the IQ and emotional control of the children at four years old (Salzwedel, Stephens, and Goldman, 2018).

"As young children develop, their early emotional experiences literally become embedded in the architecture of their brains" (National Scientific Council on the Developing Child, 2011). This means that young children's early experiences build brain structures and connections that influence emotional learning in the children's present and future.

> "A growing body of scientific evidence tells us that emotional development begins early in life, that it is a critical aspect of the development of overall brain architecture, and that it has enormous consequences over the course of a lifetime" (National Scientific Council on the Developing Child, 2011).

Later in this chapter, we will discuss what teachers can do to support infants' and toddlers' development of the emotional brain.

# Emotional Competence—
# A Key to Success in Life and School

For young children, the development of the emotional brain and the acquisition of emotional competence can have lifelong consequences. Young children's healthy and positive social and emotional skills and attitudes predict learning, academic performance, and other positive long-term outcomes (U.S. Department of Education, n.d.).

A study looked at the relationship between mothers' affection and attention levels with their eight-month-old children and the children's later levels of anxiety and hostility as adults. The researchers found that, at age thirty, the children of mothers who had provided warm and caressing affection were less anxious and hostile with others and engaged in better social interactions than the children of mothers who had provided negative attention (Maselko et al., 2011). The researchers discussed the possibility that the hormone oxytocin (sometimes known as the cuddle or hug hormone) released during moments of closeness between parents and children may have supported the neural development of the areas of the brain that support effective social interactions and mental health (Gardner, 2010).

Compared to those who are not emotionally competent, young children who are emotionally competent are more likely to experience the following:

- The ability to manage their emotions and behavior (Lindsey et al., 2009)
- Better social success and peer relations (Denham et al., 2003; Denham et al., 2016)
- Fewer behavioral challenges during the early years and in elementary school (Briggs-McGowan, 2008)
- Early school success (Denham et al., 2015)

These are powerful and life-changing outcomes that result from developing a healthy emotional brain in the first three years.

Most children will not outgrow their emotional challenges without support from caring adults. For example, research tells us that infants who withdraw from social interactions with adults and peers at one year of age experience more emotional and behavioral challenges at ages three and five years unless they experience helpful adult support (Guedeney et al., 2014). Infant and toddler teachers, then, must pay close attention to children's emotional competence remarkably early in their lives and must make the emotional development of infants, toddlers, and two-year-olds a priority in their program. Children's ability to regulate their emotions is especially important. This ability ensures children's relationship and academic success (Djambazova-Popordanoska, 2016).

# The Importance of Emotion Regulation

Emotion regulation is a critical part of emotional competence. As discussed earlier, emotion regulation involves children (and adults) learning to manage their emotions to successfully interact with others and focus on their play and work. Emotion regulation is vital for children to develop because it influences both their emotional well-being and their academic and learning success.

The ability to manage their emotions, wait patiently, and focus their attention on a task influences children's school readiness and ability to learn (Jaekel et al., 2015). Emotion-regulation skills directly affect children's moods and self-esteem, the two essential components of emotional well-being (Djambazova-Popordanoska, 2016). In almost every chapter in this book, we cite important research concerning the importance of emotion regulation for young children's emotional, social, and academic success.

# Experiences that Support Optimal Brain Development and Emotional Competence

During the first three years, as children experience the emotions of adults in their lives, they learn how to understand and express emotions. As children learn (with adult support) to express and control their emotions in healthy ways, they develop the brain capacity to regulate their emotions so that they may develop caring relationships with others.

Your interactions with infants and toddlers, then, are critical to their development. As an infant-toddler professional, you make a difference in how the architecture of the emotional brain develops. Following are proven ideas that teachers can use to support the best development of healthy emotional brain structures. We will expand on these in the chapters that follow.

## Engage in Caring Relationships with Infants and Toddlers

Caring relationships are at the heart of early brain development. "If babies' expectations for protection and nurturance are met, their brains experience pleasure and delight" (Lally and Mangione, 2017). Babies then become confident that they can get their needs met through positive relationships with others. If infants and toddlers do not get their needs met through caring relationships, their emotional and social development will suffer.

# Use Nurturing Touch, Affection, and Attention

Affection and love shape a baby's brain and are essential to brain development in the early years of life, particularly to the development of the social and emotional brain system. Affection and love are like nutrients that feed a very young child's brain and affect how the brain becomes structured. Because babies need to learn through experiences, the ways you show them to connect with others, love, and cope with stress will create lasting pathways in the brain (Gerhardt, 2014).

Touch is a powerful communicator of emotions and is important in adult-child interactions. A number of research studies have shown that babies who are touched and held more score better on developmental assessment tests in both mental and motor skills (Ardiel and Rankin, 2010). Hold and snuggle infants in response to their needs. Offer hugs to older infants and toddlers.

Share moments of pleasure with infants and toddlers. When mothers and two-month-old infants shared longer moments of pleasure, the children's social and emotional development at two years of age was better. Shared moments of pleasure at two months even protected children from parents' mental health problems (Mäntymaa et al., 2015).

# Engage in Adult-Child Synchrony and Joint Attention with Children

When caring adults interact directly with infants, infants' and adults' brains become synced and "share" experiences and responses. In a study by Piazza and colleagues, researchers asked parents to sing, read a story, and play with their nine- to fifteen-month-old infants. As they interacted, the researchers studied the infants' and parents' brain activity. When the parents engaged in mutual eye contact and shared emotions and jointly focused on an object or activity with their infants, the parents' and infants' brains began to predict what the other was going to do next. Their brain activity was linked together (Piazza et al., 2020). The strongest coupling of brain activity occurred in the prefrontal cortex, which is responsible for learning, planning, memory, and self-control. The researchers concluded that this type of adult-child sensitivity and synchrony with children's actions supports infants' emotional brain development.

In another study, researchers examined infants' and mothers' brain waves as they interacted with each other (Santamaria et al., 2019). When the mothers expressed more happy and positive emotions with their infants, including eye contact, the brain waves indicated that the babies were learning more from the adult. When you are feeling positive and happy with the children in your program, they will be more attuned to learn more from you.

Sensitive adult care for infants and toddlers, described as prompt and adequate responses to the child's signals and needs, relates to higher levels of cognitive competence. Researchers Sethna and colleagues (2017) found that parental sensitivity in early childhood is positively associated with more optimal brain development at age

eight, including a larger total brain volume, larger gray-matter volume, and thicker cortices in several areas of the brain.

When you observe infants' and toddlers' signals for when they need to be held, eat, sleep, interact more, or take a break from interacting, you are in synchrony with the children. You are supporting their structural brain development when you respond to their smiles with your smiles, look where a child is looking or pointing and talk about your shared interest, and respond to children's sounds and words with yours (Kok et al., 2015).

Of course, language and reading experiences are critical for infants' and toddlers' brain development. We emphasize this, as well as the importance of nurturing children, throughout this book.

## Experiences that Limit Emotional Brain Development and Emotional Competence

In chapters 8 and 9, we will highlight the dangers of toxic stress to young children's brain development. Poorer emotional brain-structure development can lead to emotional challenges, such as excessive anger, stress, and fear. These emotions, if not regulated, interfere with the ability to concentrate, think clearly, and make and keep friends.

Poverty can have a negative effect on infants' and toddlers' brain development, with parts of the brain that affect learning, attention, the ability to cope with stress, and behavior lagging in development (Hanson et al., 2013; Luby, 2015; Wijeakumar et al., 2019). This happens if parents are depressed or stressed and if young children experience stress, lack of sleep, poor nutrition, and less healthy stimulation. When parents were identified as nurturers, however, children were less likely to experience detrimental changes in their brains (Luby, 2015). This is crucial information for infant and toddler professionals. Nurturing young children and supporting families to nurture their children are two critically important things we can do to support young children's brain development that can have lifelong positive effects.

> Nurturing young children and supporting families to nurture their children are two critically important things we can do to support children's brain development that can have lifelong positive effects.

You can make a significant and vital difference in young children's emotional brain development. Use as many responsive, emotionally supportive ways as possible to support young children's emotional development and learning.

## Resources

The Center on the Developing Child at Harvard University offers free written resources and excellent videos: https://developingchild.harvard.edu

Healthy Baby, Healthy Brain, a website of the Best Start Resource Centre in Ontario, offers resources and interesting videos for parents and teachers: https://www.healthybabyhealthybrain.ca

# Summary

Use the following ideas from this chapter to support infants' and toddlers' emotional development.

- Notice and appreciate the emotional capabilities of infants and toddlers. They smile and your heart melts. They frown and you try to find out what is bothering them. Infants and toddlers have many emotional skills for engaging adults and peers in their emotional world.

- Help young children develop optimal brain structures that influence how they will feel and relate to others, both when they are young and when they are older. Understand how emotional development is built into the architecture of the brain.

- Recognize how emotional competence is the key to children's success in life and in school. The many aspects of emotional competence influence how children function at home, at school, and in the community.

- Appreciate how closely emotion regulation relates to young children's success in relationships with adults and peers and to their ability to focus and learn. Emotion regulation involves coregulation with you during the first three years of life, because children need adults to help them learn to manage their often challenging and confusing emotions.

- Use caring behaviors, affection, positive attention, joint attention, and sensitivity to children's needs to support young children's brain development. Stress can limit how children's brains develop. Children who experience poverty are at risk for damage to their brain development. When you nurture children, you help alleviate some of the possible detrimental effects of poverty.

# Key

# FOUR

Know How and When Children Develop
Their Emotional Skills

This chapter describes how infants' and toddlers' emotional skills and competence develop during the first three years with you.

## In this chapter you will learn:

- How, in each age group, infants and toddlers develop in the following areas:
  - » Recognizing and identifying feelings of self and others
  - » Expressing feelings
  - » Understanding what causes feelings in self and others
  - » Managing their emotions

- How emotional development is a part of the whole child

- How to observe, learn about, and support children's emotional knowledge and skills

- How to learn about development and strategies from early learning guidelines

The first three years of a child's life are busy, emotion-filled years. Incredibly, starting as early as birth, young children react to facial and body expressions of emotion in others, especially their primary caregivers. Infants and toddlers are constantly learning to recognize their own and others' emotions. As toddlers, they may be able to identify and name facial expressions such as anger, sadness, happiness, and fear. They gradually learn the words to express their own and others' emotions. Understanding what causes emotions happens in the toddler years (Fernández-Sánchez, Giménez-Dasí, and Quintanilla, 2014). Throughout the early years, young children are learning emotion regulation, the ability to manage their emotions.

# Infants

Young infants are born with the ability to learn to understand and identify the feelings of themselves and others and to express and manage their emotions. Infants are emotion readers. They tune in to the emotions expressed in a caregiver's voice, face, and body movements from very early in life. They are paying attention and can detect and feel emotional information from others.

# Recognizing and Identifying Feelings of Self and Others

Infants' ability to discriminate among emotions develops over the first year of life. Infants do not have the words for those emotional expressions that they see in their favorite caregivers, but they can distinguish among happy, sad, and fearful faces and voice tones. Even three-month-olds are sensitive to adults' emotional expressions. In one study, researchers found that when three-month-olds watched images of people who looked at new objects with either fearful or neutral facial expressions, the infants looked longer at the fearful objects than the neutral objects (Hoehl, Wiese, and Striano, 2008).

Five-month-olds can match a facial expression of emotion with a voice tone (Vaillant-Molina, Bahrick, and Flom, 2013). As mentioned earlier in this book, when researchers had five-month-old infants listen to other infant vocal expressions of happiness or joy versus anger or frustration, infants were able to look at the facial expression that matched the vocal expression. You may have observed the infants in your program listening carefully and watching when you or a peer is happy or frustrated.

These young infants also show some understanding of the meaning of an emotion expressed in another's voice, face, and body movement (Heck et al., 2018). Four- to five-month-olds react differently when they hear an approving tone versus a negative tone of voice (Castellanos, Shuman, and Bahrick, 2004). Children this age begin to react to different faces as well as voice tones. They avoid angry and fearful faces but not happy, sad, or neutral faces (Hunnius et al., 2011).

Seven-month-old infants in one study (Kobiella et al., 2008) paid more attention to angry faces than fearful faces. The authors conclude that an adult's angry face may have made the infants more uncomfortable than the fearful face. Yet fearful faces also attract seven-month-old infants' attention. Infants watched a fearful face much longer than a happy face (Peltola et al., 2015). These infants are not only tuning into the different meanings of peers' and adults' expressions of emotions but are also becoming attuned to threat (Vaish, Grossman, and Woodward, 2008). We know that too much threat in young children's lives, such as adults' angry and fearful faces or voices, can interfere with emotional development.

Infants even change their behavior based on the emotions you express. Have you ever seen an older infant look at you, listen to you, or crawl to you, her favorite teacher, when a stranger enters the room? This infant behavior is called *social referencing*. The infant looks to or listens to a trusted adult to see what emotions the adult expresses when looking at or approaching a stranger (Vaish and Striano, 2004). Your response guides the infant's behavior. If you have a happy or neutral face, the infant is likely to stay where she is, feeling unthreatened. However, infants typically avoid or withdraw from playing if the trusted adult has a negative response to a stranger (Leventon and Bauer, 2013). For example, the child may scramble quickly to your lap if she trusts you to keep her safe.

The tone of your voice and your facial expressions influence the quality of lives of infants and toddlers. They will trust you, relax with you, and emotionally connect with you when you use happy, joyful, and soothing expressions and voices when you are with them (Santamaria et al., 2019).

When infants pay attention to their peers' fearful and distressed faces, take the time to help them learn to respond to their peers with caring and sensitivity (Grossmann, Missani, and Kroi, 2018). For example, when you notice that a young infant is focusing her attention on another infant who looks fearful or distressed, say, "I see that Mario is upset. You see it too. I will help him feel happy again." If appropriate, you could take the infant with you to comfort the other baby. Encourage a crawling infant to help a distressed peer by patting her gently or giving her a blanket.

## Expressing Feelings

Babies cry! They cry when they are hungry, in pain, and tired. They may cry when a beloved parent says goodbye to them in the morning. They cry when they want and need your attention. They cry because that is their primary way to communicate that they need food, sleep, or comfort.

There are many kinds of cries. After you get to know a baby, you will begin to interpret her cries and body movements, and you will begin to more easily meet her needs. You will recognize a pain cry from a hunger cry and a tired cry from a "help me" cry. It is sometimes difficult to know exactly what causes babies to cry. However, using their clues you may be able to determine whether the crying is from anger, fear, or pain. For example, researchers Chóliz, Fernández-Abascal, and Martínez-Sánchez (2012) found that when babies between ages three and eighteen months cry from fear or anger, they keep their eyes open and their foreheads in a frown. But when babies cry from pain, their eyes remain mostly closed.

As you know, there are individual differences in how infants cry. Some babies' cries are quiet and soft, and others are quite loud. Some babies shriek, and others whimper. Each individual baby counts on you to "read" her cries and help her feel more comfortable. As infants grow during their first year, you may hear cries of protest and frustration. You may even hear a cry that sounds angry.

Because crying is a form of communication, your responses make a difference. When you respond consistently, kindly, and lovingly, the infant begins to trust you. When you carry a crying infant by holding and walking, her heart rate decreases and she is likely to become calm (Esposito et al., 2013). If you respond to infants' cries, they are more likely, as they develop, to use sounds and words to communicate their needs. Do not worry that you are "spoiling" them or reinforcing their crying when you are responsive. They desperately need you to help them meet their needs. They feel more content, satisfied, and happy and will want to communicate in ever more mature ways with you if you are responsive to their cries. You even will learn babies' sounds and body movements and often meet their needs before they cry.

Young infants do not have words, but they have sounds and body movements that tell you how they feel. When a baby begins sucking, that may be a sign that she is hungry. When another baby starts squirming, you may know her tummy is feeling upset. Older infants can learn sign language to tell you that they want *more* or *milk* or that they want to *eat*. They also engage you with their smiles.

Infants smile early and quickly learn that this is a way to engage an adult in an emotional conversation. Almost 60 percent of five hundred parents surveyed in a study of babies' smiles and laughter said that their babies' first smiles occurred at one month of age. Another 25 percent said their babies smiled by two months of age (Addyman and Addyman, 2013). Notice when infants smile, and document what causes them to smile.

Babies also laugh. Laughter is one of the first forms of language (Mireault, 2017). Everyone loves to hear an infant laugh. Of the parents surveyed in the 2013 Addyman and Addyman study mentioned above, 20 percent reported that their baby laughed by two months of age, while almost 33 percent reported that their baby laughed by three months. Babies younger than five months typically respond to social cues, such as your smile. By five months of age, babies laugh at unexpected, surprising events. For example, when an adult squishes a soft, red ball and then wears it as a nose, many five-month-olds will laugh, often uncontrollably (Mireault et al., 2018).

Babies' laughter can warm your heart. Keep a chart on the wall and document what events make infants and toddlers laugh. Encourage families to tell you what they have found that makes their babies laugh.

## Understanding What Causes Feelings in Self and Others

Older infants are beginning to understand what causes emotion (Skerry and Spelke, 2014). They may expect you to express surprise when they appear from under a blanket. They will want you to laugh when they do raspberries with their mouths. They will count on you to comfort them with a soothing look on your face when they feel sad or upset. However, they will not usually understand what makes you sad, angry, or afraid until they are older.

## Developing Emotion Regulation

Infants primarily need coregulation strategies when they are sad, angry, frustrated, or fearful (Konishi, Karsten, and Vallotton, 2018). They need you to help them become calm and feel safe. They need your arms to rock them. They need your voice to calm their crying. They need you to feed them. They need you to help them "pat gently" when touching a peer. They are, however, beginning to use some strategies to regulate emotion. Infants who become calm with you after crying are demonstrating emotion regulation. You may see infants manage their feelings by doing some of the following:

- Becoming alert and focusing on your face
- Sucking their thumbs
- Waving goodbye when a loved one leaves
- Using sign language to indicate they are hungry, want more, or are all done
- Moving away from or toward you or a peer

# Toddlers

Toddlers are constantly learning about their own and others' emotions, how to express their emotions, the causes of different emotions, and how to manage their emotions in healthy ways.

## Recognizing and Identifying Feelings of Self and Others

Toddlers and twos learn to match facial and body movements with specific emotions. For example, they have learned that certain body motions occur when someone is angry and other body motions happen when someone is fearful. Toddlers may not yet be able to say, "He's angry," but they recognize emotions by looking at others' faces and movements.

Toddlers can change their behavior based on how their peers feel. You may have seen a toddler scamper across the room to pat a friend who is crying. The toddler recognizes that the crying toddler is distressed and knows just what to do to help the upset child. The capable toddler imitates how you comfort children.

Toddlers can change their behavior based on adults' emotions too. Fifteen-month-olds in one research study (Repacholi et al., 2014) and eighteen-month-olds in another study (Repacholi and Meltzoff, 2007) watched a researcher play with a toy. After a second researcher expressed anger at the first researcher for playing with the toy, the toddlers were given a chance to play with it. Most of the toddlers would not play with the toy if the angry researcher was watching them. However, if the angry researcher left the room or looked at a magazine, the toddlers were likely to play with the toy. These toddlers not only changed their behavior based on another's emotions but also seemed to conclude, "If she can't see me doing it, she won't get angry" (Repacholi, Meltzoff, and Olsen, 2008). Toddlers tune in to others' anger. Children will watch you if you express anger to a child or another adult, and then they may be less likely to interact with you. Toddlers tend to assume that an adult who has expressed anger will become angry again (Repacholi et al., 2016). To see a video of this research, go to https://youtu.be/7FC4qRD1vn8

# Expressing Feelings

Toddlers will express many emotions with their faces, bodies, and voices. Their eyes may sparkle when they are happy. They may look surprised when a toy or peer does something new and exciting. They may even yell, "Ahh!" or "Whee!" When peers play together, they will have kinesthetic or body conversations, playing run and chase or peekaboo behind a climbing structure on the playground (Wittmer and Clauson, 2018).

Toddlers may cry often, however, if that is the only way that they can get your one-on-one attention. In the following example, Lila has learned from experience that if she cries and points to her diaper, the teacher will pay attention to her, but if she just calls the teacher with words, her teacher will not attend to her.

> Twenty-three-month-old Lila opened her eyes when she woke up from a morning nap. She started to cry loudly. When her teacher came to her crib, Lila pointed to her diaper and said, "Pee." Her teacher picked her up and took her to the changing table. We hope that Lila's teacher will begin to respond to her sounds, body movements, and words too, so that Lila doesn't have to cry to get her needs met.

Older toddlers begin to use their words and sign language to express their emotions while continuing to use gestures too. You may hear a twenty-month-old say, "Me mad," or "I no like dat." Two- to three-year-olds will say much more. For example, an almost three-year-old will talk about the emotions of a doll or stuffed animal during pretend play. While feeding a stuffed horse some pretend hay, a child might say, "The horsie is hungry and tired."

Some toddlers learn to use emotion words very effectively. They might say, "I sad," to gain the attention of a caring adult. You can admire the skills of these children to understand and express their emotions.

Older toddlers will express more emotions, such as shame, embarrassment, and guilt. In a study by Drummond and colleagues (2017), when researchers led older toddlers to believe that they had broken a researcher's toy, the toddlers showed either a guilty response or an ashamed response. The children who showed a guilty response confessed their behavior and often tried to repair the toy. The children who showed a shame-like response avoided the adult and rarely confessed or tried to make amends. The toddlers who had shown a guilty response were more likely later to help a distressed researcher than were the toddlers who showed shame. The toddlers who were more likely to show guilty behavior had experienced adults who made them feel that, although their actions were not helpful, the toddlers could make amends. The toddlers who showed shame were more likely to have experienced adults who made them feel as if they were bad, which caused toddlers to focus on themselves and their feelings rather than make amends.

## Understanding What Causes Feelings in Self and Others

In the first three years, infants and toddlers only begin to understand what may cause themselves and others to feel a certain way (Fernández-Sánchez, Giménez-Dasí, and Quintanilla, 2014). They do develop expectations for how others will feel in different situations and seem puzzled if, for example, an adult who successfully accomplishes a task begins to cry (Chiarella and Poulin-Dubois, 2013). The children expect a person to express happiness when she is successful and to be sad if she fails at a task.

## Developing Emotion Regulation

Toddlers still use many gestures to manage their strong feelings. They use fewer self-soothing strategies such as sucking their thumbs but will still use these strategies when distressed (Konishi, Karsten, and Vallotton, 2018).

Toddlers are learning strategies that help them manage their emotions and behavior. In one study in Poland (Engle and McElwain, 2011), researchers asked toddlers who sat on their parents' laps to wait 60 seconds (eighteen-month-olds) or 90 seconds (twenty-four-month-olds) for a treat in front of them. Twenty-three percent of the eighteen-month-olds waited 60 seconds, and 55 percent of the twenty-four-month-olds waited 90 seconds. The toddlers who could restrain themselves from eating the treat looked around, fidgeted, made noise, or touched themselves or their parent. They used both attention and movement to distract themselves and wait.

Toddlers still need you to help them learn strategies (coregulation) for managing and expressing their strong feelings. Toddlers demonstrate emotion regulation when they act in the following ways:

- Sucking their thumbs or stroking their faces with blankets and becoming calm when distressed

- Distracting themselves from a toy they cannot have now

- Stopping their focused play and beginning to clean up their toys, even though they are sad that they cannot continue playing

- Putting their hands behind their backs to avoid touching a forbidden object

- Paying attention while you read a story even though they are extremely excited and want to express their feelings

- Changing or eliminating the cause of their distress, such as putting a toy away in a cubbie

- Pulling a hand back from hitting a peer when angry at the peer

- Protesting to a peer with gestures, sounds, and words rather than using aggression

# Emotional Development— A Part of the Whole

Emotional development combines with other areas of development to create emotional competence. In the following example, Priya combines many skills to "read" Carlos's emotional cues and express her emotions to him.

> Priya, a two-year-old, wanted to play with Carlos, but Carlos ran away from her. Priya stood still on the playground and started to cry. Then, she suddenly stopped crying and started to run after Carlos; Priya had a plan to try to get Carlos to play with her. Carlos, who was now sitting in the sandbox, looked up as Priya exclaimed, "I sad." Priya handed Carlos a bucket and shovel and with a big smile asked, "Want pay [play]?"

In this example, Priya felt sad after Carlos rejected her. She understood that when he ran away, he did not want to play with her. He was not inviting her with his gestures to follow him. She used her thinking skills to plan to engage Carlos. She used her physical skills to run after Carlos and to give him a bucket and shovel. She used her facial expression and words to tell Carlos how she felt. She used more words to try to engage Carlos to play with her.

Emotional competence grows as cognitive, language, motor, and social development progress. Emotional development and competence may be hindered, however, when another area of development is delayed. For example, if a child's language is delayed, she may struggle to express her emotions to her peers and teachers.

Adults can help children develop emotional competence by paying attention to all the domains of development and how they interact with emotional development.

# Observing to Learn about Children's Emotional Knowledge and Skills

Adults can ask questions about children's emotional development to learn more about them. How often do they smile? What causes them to cry? The answers to these types of questions are fun to observe in young children and will provide guidance for your relationship building and curriculum planning with individual children. Family members also will love to be involved in asking and answering questions on emotional development. When involved in observing their children, family members will gain valuable insight and appreciation for their children's emotional development.

One way to gather information to learn more about each child's emotional development is to write stories about each child and keep them in the child's portfolio that is shared between home and the program. If you can, add a photo to accompany the story. The following story for Demetri highlights his emotional development.

> Today Demetri, eighteen months old, wanted to be close to Abiba. He moved near her as she was playing. Abiba looked up at Demetri and smiled. Demetri smiled back and sat down quietly beside her. He reached for a toy in front of her and then handed it to Abiba. Demetri is learning how to use his emotions (smiling) to interact successfully with other children.

The stories do not need to be long. They can capture a moment or a day in the life of a child. These stories, when collected for a child's portfolio created in a three-ring notebook, begin to show a picture of a child's emotional development. You can send a copy home so that families will know what the children in your program are learning. Families will know that you emphasize emotional development, and they will learn what to observe as well. Ask them to share with you their stories about their child's emotional growth and challenges.

Another way is to create forms for collecting information. For example, if you wanted to observe when and with whom infant smiling occurs, you could create an observation form like the one in Table 4.1.

| Name of Child | Date of Birth | Date of Smiling | Age of Child | What Caused Smiling? |
|---|---|---|---|---|
| Henry | 6/3/19 | 9/23/19 | 3 mos., 20 days | Martha (teacher) smiled at him, and he smiled back. |
| Delila | 4/5/19 | 8/5/19 | 4 mos., 9 days | She looked at Karen (teacher) and smiled. Karen smiled back. |

Following are some questions that you can answer by carefully observing young children.

- When does each baby first smile? laugh?

- What causes infants and toddlers to laugh? Is it a tickle or something surprising?

- When do babies and toddlers become angry? What causes their anger? What strategies help children express their anger in healthy ways?

- When do babies and toddlers feel sad? What causes their sadness? What comforts them?

- When do babies and toddlers feel scared? What causes their fear? What comforts them?

- How do infants and toddlers show you they are happy, sad, fearful, or angry?

As you talk with team members and families, you will brainstorm many more questions. Use the information to support young children's emotional development and learning.

# Learning about Development from Early Learning Guidelines

Most states have created early learning guidelines that inform our thinking about emotional competence, as well as the other domains of development. Created by experts in early childhood education, these guidelines outline the key indicators for children's growth and development in the early years, examples of behavior for these developmental milestones, and suggestions for supporting each indicator. For example, North Carolina's *Early Learning and Development Guidelines* (2013) describe a sequence of children's emotional developmental growth for the following areas:

- Goal ESD-6: Children identify, manage, and express their feelings.

- Goal ESD-7: Children recognize and respond to the needs and feelings of others.

North Carolina's guidelines state specifically that, for Goal ESD-6 listed above, infants will do the following:

- Express a range of emotions (happiness, sadness, fear, and anger) with their faces, bodies, and voices

- Show when they feel overwhelmed or are in distress or pain (cry, yawn, look away, extend arms or legs, arch their body, fuss)

- Soothe themselves* (suck thumb or pacifier, shift attention, snuggle with soft toy)

*The authors of this book would revise this guideline to read, "Sometimes soothe themselves but often need adults' help to become calm when distressed."

The guidelines also provide expected behaviors for younger toddlers, older toddlers, younger preschoolers, and older preschoolers. Early learning guidelines provide infant and toddler professionals with extensive information about emotional development in children's first three years of life and the strategies that support emotional learning and growth.

# Summary

Use the following ideas from this chapter to support infants' and toddlers' emotional development.

- You will find satisfaction in supporting children's learning in the following areas. You will be able to notice when children struggle with these skills and create opportunities for them to grow emotionally. Create a responsive program that supports children's learning to:

» recognize and identify feelings of self and others.

» express feelings in healthy ways.

» understand what causes feelings in self and others.

» manage (regulate) their emotions in culturally appropriate ways.

» appreciate the importance of and the amazing development of these emotional skills in young children.

- Reflect on how emotional development is a part of the whole. You can appreciate how one domain of development may affect another (for example, how delays in language may affect emotional development).

- Consistently and thoughtfully observe to learn about children's emotional knowledge and skills. You, along with families and coworkers, can ask important questions, such as, "When, with whom, and how do infants begin to express happiness?" Asking these questions and observing to answer them furthers your knowledge of emotional development.

- As you observe each individual child and your group, you will begin to understand what each child is experiencing emotionally. Writing emotional stories about each child enables you to individualize your program and share valuable information with families.

- Review the early learning guidelines in your state. Reflect on whether your program is providing opportunities for infants and toddlers to learn the important skills and knowledge identified in the guidelines.

# *Key* FIVE

## Use Relationship-Building Strategies that Support Emotional Competence

Wise infant and toddler professionals clearly understand that their professional role involves being responsive, supportive, and relationship based in care and learning programs. This is what infants and toddlers deeply need to thrive. Infants and toddlers need caring relationships that they can count on to meet their needs for safety, security, love, affection, and positive regard. Only then can they focus on loving and learning. We will explore strategies that you can use to create mutually satisfying, emotionally supportive relationships with infants and toddlers.

## In this chapter you will learn about the following ten strategies:

- Create warm, emotional connections with children.

- Use responsive and essential touch.

- Do the verbal and nonverbal dance.

- Model and encourage empathy.

- Emphasize coregulation, and teach strategies for self-regulation.

- Respond sensitively to children's distress, anger, tantrums, and negative reactions to failure.

- Practice mind-mindedness and use mentalizing strategies.

- Be physically and psychologically present.

- Be an emotional refueler.

- Use positive, gentle discipline.

## Creating Warm, Emotional Connections with Children

When children feel deeply that adults love to be with them, care about them, feel joy when they develop new skills, and value their range of emotions, they can gain emotional competence and develop to their full emotional potential. As a caregiver, you make important connections when you read young children's emotional cues, such as sadness, fear, happiness, and disgust, and respond sensitively with great care.

Young children need nourishing interactions that lead to reciprocal beneficial relationships with their special adults. When infants and toddlers experience warm, emotional relationships with their teachers, their stress hormone, cortisol, decreases across the day (Badanes, Dmitrieva, and Watamura, 2012). If young children do not experience affection from adults that they can count on, their cortisol levels rise throughout the day. Having consistently high levels or low levels of cortisol, the fight-or-flight hormone, can produce a range of detrimental health effects, including slowing a child's learning and cognitive development. High cortisol can even shrink the size of the hippocampus, a part of the brain associated with memory processing and emotion (Suor et al., 2015). Low levels of cortisol may indicate depression or hopelessness (Bergland, 2015). Reducing young children's stress levels, as Chen does in the following example, is critically important for children's healthy brain development and more.

> Teaching young and vulnerable children requires developing compassionate emotional connections with them. "The connections those emotions create profoundly affect children's lives" (Davis and Dunn, 2018).

Sarra, five months old, wakes up from her peaceful sleep crying. Her caring teacher, Chen, hears Sarra's cries and goes to her crib. Chen leans over the crib and puts her hands on Sarra's body and says softly, "I hear you crying. Sometimes it is hard to wake up alone. I want to help you feel better. I will pick you up and hold you." Sarra cuddles into Chen's body and begins to relax.

Chen helped Sarra develop emotional competence by respecting her cries as the primary way that Sarra can communicate her distress at her age. Sarra learned that when she cries, she will get her needs met. She also learned that Chen provided a safe place where she could express her emotions. As Sarra grows, she will use sounds, gestures, and words to tell Chen how she feels.

Chen had an emotional dialogue with Sarra, who shared her feelings; Chen then responded with her body and her words to help Sarra feel safe. In a dialogue, each person takes a turn in the conversation. Children who experience thoughtful and caring emotional dialogues with adults are more likely to feel securely attached to them (Hsiao et al., 2015).

In the following example, notice how Chen and Sarra shared another emotional dialogue when Sarra was two years old.

Sarra woke from her nap and hugged her stuffed bear. She called out to Chen, and Chen went to her side. Sarra looked worried. Chen tuned in to Sarra's emotions and asked, "Are you feeling worried?" Sarra nodded her head yes, even though she was just learning what the word *worried* means. Chen, staying close, said softly, "I'm here to help you. Do you want to hug your bear for a while or get up and play?" Sarra put her bear under her covers and exclaimed, "Play."

Sarra communicated her feelings with her facial expression, and Chen responded quickly by going to Sarra's side. She noticed Sarra's furrowed brow and asked if Sarra felt worried. Chen responded by comforting her and using an emotion word—*worried*. She stayed close and offered her help. Sarra felt safe, understood, and loved. Sarra responded, and the emotion dialogue continued. Chen and Sarra shared an emotional connection with each other (Saunders et al., 2015). If Chen had gone to Sarra and, without emotion, asked, "Do you want to stay on your cot or get up and play?" Sarra would not have felt the warm connection that helped her know with certainty that she could share her often conflicting emotions. Sarra was thriving because Chen was both physically and emotionally available to her.

An anchor holds a boat steady. You can be an emotional anchor for children (Dalli, 2016). You can help steady their emotions by developing a connection that promotes their trust that you will consistently and affectionately be there for them. To create warm, emotional connections with children, you can:

- create a warm, personal caring connection with each child.
- be physically and emotionally available to each child.
- engage in emotional dialogues with each child.

# Using Responsive and Essential Touch

Kind forms of touch are necessary to a child's growth and development. Frances Carlson (2006) writes about essential touch, the physical connection and comfort that is vital to infants' and toddlers' emotional well-being: "Young children need positive human touch, and lots of it, in all its forms—carrying, swinging, rolling, holding, a backrub, a hug, a pat, a high-five, rough-and-tumble play, even massage. Nurturing touch from their caregivers is essential for children to feel loved and secure . . .".

Responsive touch is touch given in response to a communication cue from children that they want and need to be held, hugged, or rocked or that they just want to be near you. You are using responsive touch when you hold a younger infant who is crying, when you hug an older infant who reaches for you with open arms, and when you welcome a toddler who wraps his arms around your leg.

In contrast, if you swoop in and hug a toddler, he may reject you. You can invite a hug by bending your knees, gazing into the child's eyes, and opening your arms. You may even ask, "Do you want a hug?" Then wait for the toddler to respond in a way that tells you whether he wants a hug.

Svinth (2018) writes about the transformative potential of nurturing touch practices in relation to toddlers' learning and emotional well-being. When Danish teachers used nurturing touch practices—such as gentle brush massage, finger massage, and body massage—with ten toddlers, the toddlers became more relaxed. Their teachers reported that nurturing touch practices enhanced their sensitivity toward the young children in their care. Nurturing touch also contributed to the children's emotional well-being. In the following example, note how Adam is better able to regulate his emotions with the help of nurturing touch.

> In our nursery we have a boy who is a year and eight months; his name is Adam. His language skills are not well developed. He has often had conflicts with the other toddlers; he would hit and bite when emotionally challenged. It was very difficult for us to help him to adjust his level of arousal when he got upset. I decided to try a new approach in order to reach him: I started to give him a finger massage. One after the other, I softly squeezed his fingers. Sometimes I would speak quietly to him during the massage; at other times, we were both silent. The encounter usually lasted around five minutes. At first, I offered him finger massage when he was calm and in a good mood, but slowly I started to offer it to him when he was tired, sad, or [upset]. After a few weeks of regular practice, he started to come to me to have his fingers massaged. Usually he didn't say anything; he just stuck his hand out in front of me. Now he sometimes approaches me even when he is tired or upset, extending his hand. I don't know exactly what he experiences, but I think the touch encounters help him cope with anger and challenging situations (Svinth, 2018).

Young children need emotionally supportive touch to survive and thrive, and this idea is supported by research. Essential, responsive, and nurturing touches change genes—important parts of our cells. In a recent study, researchers found that babies who were held and touched more than other children during their first five months had more advanced gene development at four-and-a-half years of age. The authors of the study, Groh and colleagues (2017), conclude that children with less advanced gene development may be at risk for poorer health.

To promote positive human touch, you can use essential touch, the physical connection and comfort all children need. You can use responsive touch that is in response to a child's need. And you can use nurturing touch practices that contribute to children's emotional well-being.

# Doing the Verbal and Nonverbal Dance

Doing the verbal and nonverbal dance with infants and toddlers is incredibly important for their emotional, social, cognitive, and language development. Dancing with a partner requires sensing the movements of the partner and then moving in rhythm. One leads and the other follows. In conversational dances with infants and toddlers, sometimes you lead and sometimes you follow. The baby or toddler needs to and will want to lead at times with cries, other sounds, and words. As you respond, you are helping the child become an eager communicator. Earlier in this book we talked about these dances as "serve and return." You can learn more about this at https://developingchild.harvard.edu/ guide/a-guide-to-serve-and-return-how-your-interaction-with-children-can-build-brains/

These turn-taking dances are reciprocal, with you and the child taking almost equal turns. They are mutually fulfilling, back-and-forth conversations in which each person takes a turn to keep the dance going.

These synchronized dances can be verbal or nonverbal. Shai and Belsky (2017) call the nonverbal exchanges "body-based conversations." These conversations depend on how sensitive you are to the child's emotional cues. They start when you see an infant's or toddler's body movement and figure out, based on the movement, the child's desires, thoughts, or wishes, how to sensitively respond. A baby might pull up his knees or turn away from you; a toddler may tug on your hand, scrunch up a face in disgust at a new food, or run away from you. These body movements have meaning.

> "When an infant or young child babbles, gestures, or cries and an adult responds appropriately with eye contact, words, or a hug, neural connections are built and strengthened in the child's brain that support the development of communication and social skills" (Center on the Developing Child, 2020a).

Shai and Belsky (2017) observed mothers engaging in body-based conversations with their six-month-olds. The researchers found that children whose mothers engaged the most in body-based conversations were more likely to be securely attached at both fifteen and thirty-six months; demonstrated greater socio-emotional well-being (greater peer and social competence and fewer behavior problems) at four-and-a-half years old; and demonstrated greater cognitive abilities, such as advanced language comprehension and expression, and academic skills.

One of the most important interaction strategies that adults can use with young children to enhance their well-being is to have warm, reciprocal turn-taking conversations with them (Center on the Developing Child, 2020a).

To do the verbal and nonverbal dance, you can sometimes lead and sometimes follow in your interactions with children. You can participate in both verbal and nonverbal communication with each child. And you can engage with infants and toddlers in mutually fulfilling, back-and-forth conversations.

# Modeling and Encouraging Empathy

Empathy for others may be one of the most important feelings that adults can help young children develop. Children who are able to feel empathy for others are much more likely to be successful in relationships because they truly care about others. Adult warmth and sensitivity promote young children's empathy and prosocial behavior (Spinrad and Gal, 2018). When adults respond to young children's distress, they are helping

them learn how to become calm again, modeling how to show care and concern for others, and meeting their emotional needs so that children can focus on others rather than themselves.

To encourage children to feel empathy for others, we cannot emphasize enough how important it is to label the emotions of infants and toddlers and to encourage them to talk about emotions during routines and playtime. Also, encourage toddlers to tell you how they think characters in a story are feeling. Researchers have found that toddlers aged eighteen and thirty months old, whose parents asked them to label and explain the emotions of characters in a book, helped their peers more than children of parents who did not emphasize emotions when reading to their children (Brownell et al., 2013).

To model and encourage empathy, you can be empathic with infants and toddlers. Try to imagine how they might be feeling. Be warm, loving, caring, and kind with young children. You can model care and concern for other children. You can talk with children about the specific feelings of other children and why other children may be feeling the way they do. You can encourage toddlers to help another toddler in distress by taking the distressed toddler a tissue or a toy. You can encourage a child to problem solve how to help another child. And you can label the feelings of characters in a book for infants and encourage toddlers to think about how characters are feeling.

# Emphasizing Coregulation and Teaching Strategies for Self-Regulation

As we've discussed previously, young children need your presence and coregulation strategies to help them express and control their emotions so that they can tell you how they feel in healthy ways. When children can begin to manage their emotions, they are better able to learn, concentrate on important tasks, relate to others, and make friends. Notice the coregulation strategies that Lamar's teacher uses to support Lamar's emotional growth.

> Nine-month-old Lamar's teacher, Laura, watched him drop a toy on his foot and heard him burst into loud crying. Laura walked quickly over to him, crouched down to his eye level, and said in a comforting voice, "I saw you drop the toy on your foot. That must have surprised and hurt you. Do you want me to rub your foot to make it feel better?" After rubbing Lamar's foot gently, Laura asked, "How does your foot feel now?" Lamar plopped into her lap and began sucking his thumb. After Lamar felt better, Laura asked him if he was ready to play with some playdough.

Laura helped Lamar understand that caring adults and peers will help him when he is upset. She also taught him that he could feel better if he redirected his attention from his foot to playing. First, however, she comforted him.

Respond quickly and kindly to infants' and toddlers' distress. Young children learn that with caring, soothing adults, they can begin to quiet and become peaceful again (Mirabile et al., 2009). They know that someone they trust will help them manage their often difficult-to-control feelings.

You will not "spoil" a child when you calmly comfort a child who cries or tugs at your pants leg when upset. Instead, you will help him feel how to become calm and then focus his attention on interesting activities. You will help him gain trust in caring and responsive adults.

Moreover, children whose parents coach them about emotions are able to regulate their emotions more successfully than those whose parents do not coach their children about emotion (Morris et al., 2017; Ornaghi et al., 2019). A coach teaches new skills, gives children an opportunity to practice these skills, and encourages them often.

To emphasize coregulation and teach strategies for self-regulation to infants, you can appreciate their self-soothing strategies (sucking their thumbs). Try to figure out individualized, comforting, and responsive ways to soothe each infant's crying. After comforting their distress and showing empathy for their frustration or anger, help them recover by focusing their attention on others or activities.

To emphasize coregulation and teach strategies for self-regulation to toddlers and twos, you can appreciate when they use emotion-regulation strategies, such as stopping playing to come inside, stopping themselves from taking a toy from someone, or becoming calm for nap time. With distressed toddlers, you can use a calm, soothing voice to help them become relaxed. When caring adults acknowledge what a child is feeling, the child feels heard. You can label children's emotions often. When toddlers know words for emotions, they are better able to manage their emotions and behaviors.

# Responding Sensitively to Children's Distress, Anger, Tantrums, and Negative Reactions to Failure

When you are developing strong, caring relationships with infants and toddlers, they must deeply feel that you are there to help them and not punish them when they feel distressed. Teach children what to do with the emotions they feel. You are their guide. For example, constantly say what you want them to do. If a child hits another child for taking his toy, teach them both how to use sign language or words. Teach toddlers how to cooperate and use problem-solving strategies.

If adults respond to distress with anger or punishment, children do not learn how to calm themselves. Toddlers who experience angry adult responses to their frustrations, hurts, and tantrums have a challenging time controlling their strong emotions of anger and frustration later in preschool and beyond (Mirabile et al., 2009; Sullivan and Carmody, 2018). This may be because they are imitating the angry behavior of adults or feel anger in response to harsh punishment.

Ignoring and not reacting when a child is upset may lead to the toddler escalating his behavior to get attention (Groh et al., 2017; Ornaghi et al., 2019). Ignoring children's distress does not help them learn strategies to manage their strong feelings. When having a tantrum, the toddler feels out of control. In a calm voice, you can acknowledge his frustration and give strategies for safely controlling those frustrations as illustrated by Brett in the following example.

> Mack, twenty-three months old, threw himself on the ground outside and kicked
> his feet wildly while screaming, "I want the wagon!" His teacher, Brett, lowered

himself to the ground and said calmly, "I hear you. You really want the wagon. Marla is playing with it right now. When she finishes playing with it, I will help you have a turn with the wagon. Do you want to come sit on my lap until she finishes her turn with the wagon?" Mack continued crying for a minute and then slowly crawled over to sit on Brett's lap.

It can be difficult to control our own emotions when an infant will not stop crying or a toddler is incredibly angry and hurts others or materials. Yet if we cannot control our anger, how can we expect infants and toddlers to control theirs? Harsh reactions can lead to children experiencing behavior challenges (Crandall et al., 2018). Punishment is related to social withdrawal and anxiety, especially for boys who often feel angry or sad (Engle and McElwain, 2011). Boys may need extra emotional-coaching support.

It is easy to think that infants and toddlers are trying to manipulate us when they cry or have a tantrum. However, it is important to think of these emotional displays as genuine expressions of feelings. Brophy-Herb and colleagues (2009), after interviewing Early Head Start parents, found that more empowered parents view themselves as role models, and reflective parents consider themselves guides for helping young children become aware of their own and others' emotions. Role models are constantly aware of how their children imitate their behavior. They continually and thoughtfully model how they want their children to express emotions. Reflective parents think about the meaning of children's emotional expressions, label expressions with their children, and engage in sensitive interactions to guide children's healthy emotional understanding and expression. The children of adults who consider themselves reflective role models are more likely to manage their challenging emotions in healthy ways.

To respond sensitively to children's distress, anger, tantrums, and negative reactions to failure, you can respond with words and ideas about how to express anger in healthy ways. You can avoid responding to children's emotional outbursts with your own anger. Instead, reflect on children's emotions that challenge your emotions. You can consider yourself an important role model for children on how to manage their challenging emotions, and constantly help them express and manage their emotions in healthy ways by emphasizing and encouraging specific positive behavior.

# Using Mind-Mindedness and Mentalizing Strategies

You may have heard the term *mindfulness*, meaning nonjudgmental awareness of one's own feelings, thoughts, and environment in a given moment. The term *mind-mindedness* (Meins, 2013; Meins et al., 2013; Shai and Meins, 2018) refers to adults being aware of young children's spoken and often unspoken thoughts, emotions, and goals—in other words, their minds. To use mind-mindedness, try to put yourself in children's minds to understand what they are thinking, as Jelani's teacher does.

> As eight-month-old Jelani crawled toward a toy that he spotted across the room, the teacher commented, "You really want that car. You are crawling fast."

The term *mentalizing* means "to be attuned to the baby's mind" (Zeegers et al., 2018). Mentalizing refers to adults' ability to interpret young children's nonverbal cues, such as their body postures, facial expressions, and quality of movement (Shai and Belsky, 2017). Researchers Shai and Belsky found that parents' use of mentalizing with their six-month-old infants predicted attachment security at fifteen and twenty-six months and predicted language abilities, academic skills, behavior problems, and social competence at fifty-four months. Your attunement to a baby's mind is a powerful way to support infants' emotional and social development, including self-regulation skills (Senehi, Brophy-Herb, and Vallotton, 2018).

To practice mind-mindedness and use mentalizing strategies, you can respond to infants' and toddlers' verbal cues about what they need and how they are feeling. Also, you can figure out the desires, thoughts, and wishes of infants and toddlers by their nonverbal cues, such as their facial expressions and body movements. For example, if an infant arches his back away from you, you know that the baby is overwhelmed with stimulation. You can comment on what you think may be his needs and goals. Children will let you know if you guessed wrong. Then try again to "read a child's mind."

# Being Physically
# and Psychologically Present

You can be physically present but psychologically absent for a young child. Or, you can be both physically and psychologically present. Physical presence means that you are near a child and physically able to meet his needs. Psychological presence means that your eyes, ears, body, and attention are available to a child. In a study of toddlers in child care, teachers ignored toddlers' bids for attention around 50 percent of the time. The teachers were physically present but not psychologically available to the toddlers. Some toddlers persisted at getting attention; however, some gave up quickly when their teacher did not respond (Honig and Wittmer, 1985).

Infants and toddlers are more likely to have social and emotional challenges when their mothers are psychologically absent (Bocknek et al., 2012). If infants or toddlers experience this absence from teachers in their program, they may be at further risk for difficulty with creating satisfying relationships with adults, emotion regulation, and peer success.

You cannot always respond to a young child's need for you. However, you can smile at the child and say, "As soon as I'm finished changing Matt's diaper, I will come to you." Or, you can say, "Wait here by me and I will listen to you as soon as I can." These kind words will help a young child not only to feel valued but also to learn to wait just a bit; that is, building self-regulation. Infants and toddlers may not be able to understand all these words. However, they will know that you are a trustworthy adult who will attend to their needs when you can.

To be physically and psychologically present, you can be on children's body- and eye-level as often as possible. You can look at a child when he wants your attention. You can respond, even if it is to say to an infant, "I hear you. You are hungry. I am getting your bottle right now." Respond, even if it is to say to a toddler, "I will be there in a minute. Come stand by me while you wait."

# Being an Emotional Refueler

Infants and toddlers often need emotional refueling (Kaplan, 1998; Mahler, Pine, and Bergman, 1973). Just as a car needs fuel to run, young children need their emotional selves filled by you. An infant may crawl into your lap as you sit on the floor. He needs your cuddles, hugs, and smiles to refuel emotionally and then go forth with energy and vigor. An older infant learning to walk will need emotional refueling often as he takes a few steps, splats down on his bottom, and then gets up to start trying again. If you are emotionally and physically available, the newly walking infant may plop down in your lap, sometimes not even looking back to make sure you are there. A toddler with whom you have a good relationship may be off exploring and suddenly realize that he needs to emotionally check in with you. Often, the toddler will stay by your side, basking in your attention, for only a few minutes before running off again. On days when a toddler is emotionally depleted, he may stay by you all day.

To be an emotional refueler, you can sit on the floor often, so that crawling infants and toddlers know that you are physically and emotionally available. When they come to you smiling or crying, you can welcome them back from their explorations to let them know that they have someone who really cares about them. You can notice what their faces and bodies tell you about their need to rest by you or when they need a hug.

# Using Positive, Gentle Discipline

Positive, gentle discipline is adults' use of supportive and kind teaching and problem-solving discipline. It includes the following:

- Being responsive to children's interests
- Listening to children and commenting on their feelings
- Giving reasons to toddlers for why they should (or should not) behave in a certain way
- Problem solving with children

You can start problem solving with older infants and young toddlers by giving them choices. With toddlers, you can ask for their ideas on how to solve a problem.

Several research studies have concluded that positive discipline results in children's increased emotional and social skills, including self-regulation (LeCuyer and Houck, 2006; Song et al., 2018). Negative discipline includes hostility, anger, and overcontrolling (Song et al., 2018) and contributes to a lack of self-regulation in children.

Fifteen-month-old Joaquin used his newly found walking speed to cross the room and take a brightly colored truck out of fourteen-month-old Rolf's hands. Joaquin's and Rolf's teacher Amy watched to see what would happen. Rolf started crying loudly as Joaquin sped back across the room. Amy went to Joaquin, bent down on his level, and said, "You really like that truck." Joaquin nodded his head yes. Amy pointed at Rolf, who was being comforted by another teacher, and said, "Rolf is crying because you took his truck. He is sad now. He really liked the truck too." Amy gently put out her hand for Joaquin to take and said, "Let's go help Rolf." After crossing the room, Amy pointed to Joaquin and then to herself and said, "Would you like to give the truck back to Rolf or would you like for me to give it back? We can get that big blue truck on the floor [pointing to another truck])." Joaquin, eager to get the big blue truck, handed the first truck to Rolf. After helping Joaquin notice how happy Rolf was to get his truck back, Amy then encouraged the two boys to push their trucks together across the floor.

Notice that Amy commented on both Joaquin's and Rolf's feelings. Because Joaquin knew from experience that Amy was not going to punish him, he listened to her. She offered him a choice while also pointing out another truck. Enticed by the new truck, Joaquin gave Rolf's truck back to him. Amy asked Rolf if he was feeling better and encouraged Joaquin to notice how happy Rolf was now. Amy tried to help Joaquin and Rolf restore their relationship by encouraging them to push their trucks together.

If Joaquin had refused to give the truck to Rolf, Amy would have continued encouraging him to notice how Rolf was feeling. She would have held out her hand for Joaquin to give her the truck. If Joaquin refused again, Amy, who knows how hard it is for toddlers to let go of a prized possession, would have picked up the blue truck and asked Joaquin to hold it. He then would have likely let go of the truck that Rolf wanted. Amy knows that this type of discipline takes more time than if she had snatched the truck from Joaquin and given it back to Rolf. She also knows that in that approach, Joaquin then would think about his own loss and not about Rolf's feelings.

To use positive, gentle discipline, state directions in a positive way; for example, say, "Please walk," instead of "Don't run." Use specific words to encourage and appreciate the efforts of infants and toddlers such as, "You touched her gently," or "You picked up all the blue blocks. Thank you." Be responsive to children's interests, and listen to them and comment on their feelings. Give toddlers reasons for why they should (or should not) behave in a certain way, and engage children in problem solving with you.

Crying and Laughing: The Emotional Development of Infants and Toddlers

# Summary

Use the following ideas from this chapter to develop critically important, caring relationships with infants and toddlers.

- Send a newsletter home to families to share with them why positive, caring relationships are so important for infants and toddlers and the strategies you are using to develop these relationships. Discuss how infants and toddlers need to experience affection, emotional connections, and a sense of security to survive and thrive emotionally. Send the list of ten strategies home for families.

- Use the list of strategies in this chapter as a tool for reflection. With your coteachers, reflect on how you use the ten strategies and how individual children respond to these strategies.

- Create a chart of the strategies and approaches described in each of the ten relationship-based strategies in this chapter. Place the chart on the wall in your room or family child-care home. Reflect on whether you use these strategies in your program and how you can improve your use of them.

# Key SIX

Use Teacher-Child Interaction Strategies
to Build Emotional Competence

In chapter 5 we discussed how nurturing relationships with young children help them thrive. These nurturing relationships are created from your sensitive and responsive moment-to-moment interactions with the children in your care. Your day-to-day kind and encouraging interactions support young children's emotional competence (Mortensen and Barnett, 2015, 2016). Here, we will explore effective, responsive teacher-child interaction strategies that support young children's emotional development.

## In this chapter you will learn the following ten strategies:

- Be an emotion detector, sensitively attuned and contingently responsive.

- Model a variety of emotions (in an authentic way).

- Help children read the emotions of others.

- Develop children's healthy emotional expression.

- Always acknowledge children's feelings— do not minimize feelings.

- Use emotional talk and emotion bridging.

- Emphasize causes of emotions.

- Evaluate the quality of your facial expressions and tone of voice.

- Teach and use sign language and gestures to express emotions.

- Avoid overprotecting or overreacting; manage your own emotions.

These emotionally satisfying interactions promote infants' and toddlers' emotion regulation, well-being, and health (Mortensen and Barnett, 2019).

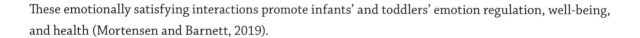

Crying and Laughing: The Emotional Development of Infants and Toddlers

# Being an Emotion Detector, Sensitively Attuned and Responsive

To be sensitively attuned and contingently responsive to the children in their care, adults first need to become emotion detectors. Emotion detectors hone their skills at understanding what each child's facial, body, and vocal cues mean for how that child is feeling. You give each child a great gift when you observe her cues and respond contingently, based on what she is trying to communicate. You build a child's sense of security when you listen and respond. The infant or toddler learns to trust that you will meet her needs and will communicate with more developmentally advanced cues as she grows.

At first you may have to guess the meaning of a baby's scrunched-up face or a toddler's sudden tears. You will try different strategies until one works. As you come to know each child better, you will be able to "read" their emotional cues more quickly. While there are universal ways that infants and toddlers show anger, for example, you will still need to attempt to determine the causes of the child's anger and the strategies that will work with her.

When you contingently respond to a child's emotional cues, you model how to interact with others. You are present, make eye contact, listen attentively, and talk with a child. You model empathy, interest, and kindness (Brophy-Herb et al., 2011), and this teaches children how to interact with others. When you respond sensitively, infants and toddlers develop expectations that social interactions will be positive (Mcquaid, Bibok, and Carpendale, 2009). They feel that they can express their feelings and that others will care.

To be an emotion detector, sensitively attuned and contingently responsive, you can observe each child's facial and body cues for expressing hunger, fear, happiness, and sadness. You can respond sensitively: kindly, thoughtfully, and in a reflective way. You know that you may guess wrong many times as you try to interpret a child's emotions, but you can keep trying. As you come to know each child, you will be better able to "read" that child's emotions and can respond based on her expressed needs.

# Modeling a Variety of Emotions in an Authentic Way

Older infants and toddlers are incredibly skilled imitators. One research study found that young toddlers (fourteen months old) were able to observe a behavior and then use that behavior later. This is called *deferred imitation* (Meltzoff, 1985, 2011). Children are watching you and their peers and learning how to express emotions. Demonstrate for young children that you have some of the same feelings they do. You might say, "I get frustrated sometimes too. When I get frustrated, I stop, take a deep breath, and try again. Do you want to try that?" Talk about your feelings as you are experiencing them with children, such as, "I get so excited when we get to play with the water table, and sometimes it feels hard to wait for it to be set up! When I have to wait, I often sing a song to myself or count my fingers. Let's count our fingers together while we wait."

In another study about young children imitating adults, researchers noted that toddlers (eighteen months old) were more likely to imitate an adult who correctly said the names of objects and were less likely to imitate an adult who incorrectly named objects, for example, calling a bird an apple (Brooker and Poulin-Dubois, 2013). Toddlers were also more likely to imitate and eat a puppet's choice of food if the puppet had been helpful to another distressed puppet. The toddlers were much less likely to imitate and eat a puppet's choice of food if the puppet had harmed another puppet. Considering these findings, one wonders if a toddler who sees you show anger toward another child will be unwilling to imitate you.

Researchers Schoppmann, Schneider, and Seehagen (2019) wanted to know whether toddlers could learn to control their emotions. An adult in the experimental group modeled for toddlers how to wait in a frustrating situation (waiting to play with a toy). The adult pretended to want a toy on a shelf but had to wait until a light under the shelf turned green. The adult modeled playing while waiting and talked about how it helped to play when frustrated and waiting for a treat or to play with a toy. The toddlers in this group were better able to use distraction through play to wait in a later frustrating situation than toddlers who had not seen an adult model how to wait.

This is powerful and valuable information. You can model for toddlers how to control challenging emotions when they must wait, are angry, or feel sad. Schoppmann, Schneider, and Seehagen (2019) emphasized that modeling for children how to manage their emotions could prevent them from experiencing behavior challenges, both now and in the future.

To help them manage their emotions, you can recognize how important modeling healthy emotional expression is for infants and toddlers. You can recognize that treating them kindly will result in their imitating your healthy emotional expression. You can constantly and carefully model the behaviors that you would like to see in children. You can model for children how to wait, such as by singing songs while waiting for lunch or to go outside. You can play with toys if a toddler is anxious about a parent returning at the end of the day. Through these behaviors, you will be modeling how to distract themselves if they have to wait.

# Helping Children Read the Emotions of Others

Just as adults read and respond to young children's emotional cues, they also want them to learn to read the cues of others. One of the most important strategies that you can use to help children read and understand the emotions of others is to teach emotion words. One study with young children demonstrated that toddlers who knew the words for *happy* and *sad* were better able to see the differences when shown a happy face and a sad face than toddlers who did not have these emotion words in their vocabulary (Lee, Besada, and Rutherford, 2018).

To help children read the emotions of others, you can point out and talk about your own emotions. Point to your happy face and say, "I feel happy." You can point out and talk about each child's emotions. When you see a child's sad face, say, "Your face tells me that you feel sad."

You can point out and talk about others' emotions. For example, you could say, "I think Michael feels angry. His face and his body tell me he is angry."

## Developing Children's Healthy Emotional Expression

Infants and toddlers often express their emotions in nonverbal ways. You support young infants' emotional expression by commenting on their emotions when they express them without words. When an infant or toddler cries or sadly sits away from others, you could say, for example, "I know it makes you sad when mommy leaves. She will be back right after your nap. You can tell me, 'I am so sad.'" Wait and comfort the child. Then ask, "Would you like to go feed the fish?"

Recognize when an infant or toddler is using her emotions to build or continue a relationship with you. Remember, toddlers use more sad faces with their mothers than they do with others, possibly because they know this will elicit support (Buss and Kiel, 2004). Are the toddlers in your program expressing sadness to elicit your attention?

Many young children find it difficult to verbally express their feelings. First, they must name a feeling as different from other feelings. To help children name feelings, read storybooks with characters who feel different emotions and comment on the faces the character makes as you talk about how that character is feeling.

To develop children's healthy emotional expressions, you can find posters of children expressing different emotions and talk with the children in your care about what those children are feeling.

You can create a feelings chart for toddlers to use when they arrive in the morning. A feelings chart has pictures or photos of children expressing different emotions. Children can point to, turn an arrow to, or place their picture by the facial expression that demonstrates how they are feeling. You can take photos of infants and toddlers in your program expressing different emotions and display them on the children's level or create a book about emotions. You can provide dolls with different expressions on their faces, then encourage toddlers to tell you how the doll feels today.

# Acknowledging Feelings

Adults minimize children's feelings when they say, "Don't cry," "Don't be a baby," or "You aren't hurt." Teachers and parents minimize toddlers' feelings when they ignore sadness, fear, or anger or say, for example, "There's nothing to be afraid of. It is just a dog." All children and adults are entitled to their feelings. They feel the way they do and will not stop feeling that way just because someone tells them to stop.

When adults minimize young children's feelings, they are creating a barrier to learning about a child. They are also dampening a child's emotional and social development (King and La Paro, 2018). An infant who is angry will not learn strategies for expressing that anger if an adult ignores the infant's angry expression. Instead, acknowledge feelings, as in the following example.

> Marta, eight months old, was sitting on the floor trying to reach some hanging bells that she could pat and ring. She looked frustrated and angry because she was having difficulty getting to a standing position. Her teacher, Ray, moved closer to Marta and commented, "I'm sorry. You cannot reach the bells. That must feel so frustrating!" Marta looked at Ray. Ray lowered the bells so Marta could reach them. A smile came over Marta's face.

When you acknowledge children's feelings, you are showing them that you recognize how they are feeling. You name the feeling. For example, you can say to a toddler who is crying because another toddler took his toy, "You are feeling sad and angry. Take my hand and we will talk to Maurice."

Sometimes, it is difficult to understand which underlying feeling a child is experiencing. For example, a toddler who withdraws from others may be fearful. You may be able to detect the fear by her quick, darting glances around the room as if checking for danger.

To support children's feelings, you can recognize that infants and toddlers will express their sadness, anger, and fear in a variety of ways and with different intensities. You can consistently acknowledge their feelings before acting upon them. You can actively listen to what a baby or toddler is trying to express to you. This will become a wonderful habit that often defuses a challenging situation and will help you stop and reflect on the child's perspective. This strategy is one of the most important techniques to use to help young children understand their own and others' emotions and feel compassion for others. You are constantly modeling the words to use to express their feelings, and you are modeling empathy for others' feelings. Infants and toddlers will respond to the warmth of your words and know that you truly understand how they feel. You can teach them ways to express their emotions, such as using sign language and gestures.

# Using Emotion Talk and Emotion Bridging

When you use emotion talk and emotion bridging, you help infants and toddlers learn words to express their emotions. Emotion talk involves using words as often as possible when with children. Use the words *happy, sad, angry, afraid, frustrated,* and other words, even with young infants. Use them throughout the day in all activities: at lunchtime, when you are outdoors, during story time, or when you are changing a diaper. "Over time, these mini-conversations translate into a rich body of experiences for the child" (Brophy-Herb et al., 2015). Emotion bridging involves not only labeling an emotion but also putting it into context, as in the following example.

> In a storybook being read to a toddler, the character in the story lost her bird. The teacher said, "She's sad because she lost her bird," and then the teacher tied this back to the child's life. "Remember when you lost your bear and you were sad?" (Michigan State University, 2015).

Your use of emotion talk and emotion bridging helps young children manage the emotions that challenge them. In a research study, toddlers who were at risk for early behavioral problems benefited when their mothers used emotion talk. Toddlers who learned words to express emotions, needs, and wishes were more likely to use these words rather than use aggression or express their frustration by having a tantrum (Brophy-Herb et al., 2015).

Infants and toddlers benefit in additional ways when you use emotion talk and emotion bridging. They learn novel words and increase their overall vocabulary. Toddlers with better language skills that increase over time use their language to support and distract themselves when upset rather than show their anger (Roben, Cole, and Armstrong, 2013). Twenty-four-month-olds with larger vocabularies do better both academically and behaviorally when they enter kindergarten than do peers with smaller vocabularies (Morgan et al., 2015).

To support emotion talk and emotion bridging, you can use emotion words often and help toddlers label their emotions. You can play emotion games, such as asking everyone to make a sad face, then a happy face, then a frightened face. You can use emotion-bridging strategies by putting the emotion in context. You can talk with families about the culturally relevant emotion words that they use. If a child is learning English as a second language, you can learn and use words for emotions in the child's primary language.

# Emphasizing the Causes of Emotions

Young children's understanding of what behaviors cause others to be happy, sad, angry, or afraid develops over the first three years through their experience with others. You enhance their learning when you use emotion words and when you talk about the causes of emotions. It is not too early to start with infants, as you can see in the following example.

> Kathryn, an infant teacher, holds three-month-old Elizabeth, who is crying. Beta, nine months old, crawls over to Kathryn, looking distressed. Kathryn leans down to talk to Beta and in a calm, soothing voice says, "Are you worried about Elizabeth? She is crying because she is hungry. Would you like to come with me to get her bottle of milk?"

You can emphasize causes of children's behavior whenever a child expresses an emotion. In the following example, Marco's teacher uses emotion words often and tries to emphasize what causes children's emotions.

> Out on the playground, Tahani, twenty-seven months old, started crying. Marco looked concerned as he watched Tahani. The children's teacher said calmly to Marco, "Tahani seems sad and is crying because someone accidentally stepped on her toes. How can we help Tahani be happy again?" as they walked over to Tahani.

To help children understand the causes of emotions, you can talk about why a child may feel sad, angry, frustrated, or fearful. This is often your best guess as to the reasons that contributed to the child's feelings.

You can encourage toddlers to tell you what happened when you see them crying or angry. Simply ask, "Oh, what happened?" Although older toddlers may begin to ask many "Why?" questions, it is difficult for older toddlers to answer the question, "Why are you crying?"

# Evaluating the Quality of Your Facial Expressions and Tone of Voice

Your face and voice teach infants and toddlers about emotions. As you play interactive, reciprocal sound games, they are watching your face and listening to your voice. They are figuring out what facial expressions match different voice tones. By five months of age, infants can hear an angry or frustrated infant voice or a happy or joyful voice and then look at the appropriate picture of an infant face that matches that voice (Vaillant-Molina, Bahrick, and Flom, 2013).

> "Faces are quite special for infants right from birth"
> (LoBue, 2016).

Your facial expressions strongly communicate to children how they should feel about themselves. As they investigate your face, they see your approval or disapproval of them. Your smiles light up their moments and days and tell them that you value them. Your laughter communicates to them that you enjoy being with them.

Your warm looks of support emotionally sustain them and build their strong and healthy sense of self-worth. With your face, you have the power to build young children's sense of who they are.

Your voice carries messages of approval and disapproval too. Does your voice soothe a crying infant? Does the tone of your voice convey respect or disrespect for children? Young children prefer to listen to happy-sounding voices. Happy-sounding speech has a higher tone, a rapid rate, and more variation from high notes to lower notes (Corbeil, Trehub, and Peretz, 2013). Infants four to thirteen months of age prefer happy-sounding talk and singing to neutral voices. They listened longer to happy-sounding talk directed at them than they did to an adult humming with them (Corbeil et al., 2013). However, when they are sad, your sad voice and face can tell them that you understand their feelings.

You can show your approval of children with your face and voice. Smile often with infants and toddlers. Engage in pleasant one-on-one eye contact, and use a sincere, warm, and kind tone of voice.

# Teaching and Using Sign Language and Gestures to Express Emotions

Before infants and toddlers can talk, they are telling you how they feel. Because infants' motor skills develop before their ability to say words, they often communicate their emotions with gestures and sign language. Researcher Claire Vallotton (2008) observed infants from nine to thirteen months of age communicating the emotions *happy, mad, sad*, and *scared* in a child-care program. She shared the following example.

> Cathy (eleven months old) picked up a small stuffed-animal spider from the floor and looked at it for a while. She looked at her caregiver and said, "Me!"
>
> Her caregiver replied, "Yeah, you are holding a spider, Cathy." Cathy looked at the spider and pounded her fist on her chest (the gesture for *scared*). Then, she looked back at the caregiver, who said, "It seems that you are telling me that you are scared of the spider." Cathy nodded without a smile.

Cathy showed her emotions by using a *scared* gesture. She nodded to show her agreement. Her unsmiling face communicated her scared feelings. At other times, Cathy showed that she was sleepy, sad, or angry with gestures.

Some children learn sign language quickly and use it often. Others use their own creative gestures rather than official sign language. Because children's motor skills develop before their complex language skills, using signs and gestures can be a powerful way for them to communicate with the important adults in their lives. In a study by Konishi, Karsten, and Vallotton (2018), when teachers demonstrated and used sign language and gestures in a program for eleven- to twenty-eight-month-olds, the toddlers learned to use sign language and gestures to regulate their emotions, especially when they were distressed.

In another study, researchers observed toddlers at fourteen, sixteen, and eighteen months of age to learn how young children use gestures to support their self-regulation (Basilio and Rodriguez, 2017). The authors of the study found that "toddlers think with their hands" during play with toys. These toddlers used many gestures, such as the following:

- Handing a toy to a parent
- Asking a parent for help by reaching out to the parent
- Clapping for self and a parent to show happiness
- Smiling at a parent to share an experience
- Pointing at a toy
- Showing a toy to a parent
- Giving a toy to a parent

When the gestures were acknowledged by parents as legitimate communication, parents responded and took interaction turns with the children. As we know, this responsiveness and turn-taking build young children's desire and skills to communicate effectively with others.

To help infants and toddlers communicate their emotions with gestures, you can learn sign language for key emotions, such as *sad, happy,* and *angry*. Use sign language with the vocal word. You can work with family members to teach them some key signs or gestures. You can observe and chart all the ways that infants and toddlers in your program express emotions nonverbally. And you can respond promptly to their gestures and signs.

# Avoiding Overprotecting or Overreacting

Adults usually want to protect infants and toddlers from harm. However, when adults' protective behavior keeps children from doing an activity that they can do (or do with support), they become more sad, fearful, and stressed (Hutt, Buss, and Kiel, 2013). Our own experiences may influence why we overprotect children, giving them the impression that the world is a dangerous place. To avoid overprotecting children in your program, assess a situation, such as using a slide, with your coworkers. Ask how the activity could be made safe for children of a certain age. Precaution is important. Overprotectiveness, however, may dampen young children's sense of self-efficacy and increase their fear of new experiences. Infants and toddlers must feel safe to learn as they try new activities that entice them to creatively explore materials, places, peers, and equipment. Overprotecting by constantly saying, for example, "Watch out," or "Be careful," makes children feel that the world is a dangerous place. Instead, teach them how to use new materials and equipment safely in specific ways. For example, teach toddlers to climb up the steps of a slide while holding on to the railings.

Overreacting to children's behavioral issues, such as hitting by yelling, scolding, and using time-out, results in children who are less kind and helpful (Xiao, Spinrad, and Carter, 2018).

> Kylo (twenty-nine months old) ran across the room and hit Rey (thirty months old) on the head with an aluminum pie tin that he found in the dramatic-play area. Frankie, their toddler teacher, ran across the room and exclaimed to Kylo, "That was bad. You come with me and sit by your cubby and think about what you did." Kylo started to cry.

In this example because the teacher yelled, scolded, and used time-out, Kylo focused on himself and his own feelings rather than on Rey's feelings. Kylo did not learn any new strategies to manage his anger. He did not learn how to initiate play with another toddler with kind and helpful strategies. Instead, he sat alone and cried, feeling sad.

To avoid overprotecting and overreacting, you can reflect on your fears and how they influence how you interact with children. You can work with coteachers to create safe, fun, interesting, and challenging environments that encourage children to take safe risks as they play. You can reflect on children's behaviors that make you angry, frustrated, or sad and the strategies you can use when children hurt themselves and others.

# Summary

Use the following ideas from this chapter to interact in ways that support infants' and toddlers' emotional development.

- Share with families the ten adult-child interaction strategies that you are using to support infants' and toddlers' emotional development and why they are important for children's emotional health.
- Reflect on the ten strategies with your coteachers. To improve your practice, choose one strategy each week to emphasize.
- Reflect on each child's emotional experiences. Ask questions such as:

  » What are the emotional experiences of infants and toddlers from the child's perspective?

  » Do infants feel as if their feelings are important to you?

  » Do infants and toddlers feel that you understand their anger, sadness, joy, and fears and help them manage these emotions in healthy ways?

» Do they see and hear you consistently, kindly, and actively listen to their overt and subtle expressions of emotions?

» Do they feel that they can express the challenging and often contradictory feelings they experience each day and that they can trust you to value all their emotions?

# Key SEVEN

Craft an Emotionally Rich, Caring
Curriculum and Environment

This chapter emphasizes the setting in which the ten relationship-based practices and the ten responsive teacher-child interaction strategies occur each day.

## In this chapter you will learn about the following:

- Developing your relationship-based philosophy

- Creating a relationship-based program

- Helping children feel a sense of belonging

- Recognizing that infants and toddlers are active learners

- Setting up a responsive curriculum

- Developing an emotionally responsive curriculum

- Setting up an emotionally responsive environment

- Using emotional activities each day

- Using routines as a time to build relationships

- Reading books and singing songs about emotions

- Encouraging family members to read storybooks about emotions with children

- Creating a social-emotional activity (SEA) for the week

# Developing Your Relationship-Based Philosophy

A program philosophy includes your beliefs about what children need and what strategies promote and support children in flourishing. A philosophy guides how you interact with children and how you set up your program to meet the needs of infants and toddlers.

Because we know that every child needs to experience positive, caring, loving, and consistent relationships with teachers, family members, and other adults, we support a relationship-based philosophy for teachers of young children. Infants and toddlers urgently and consistently need nourishing, caring, and thoughtful interactions with teachers in order to thrive. Loving relationships among teachers, children, and peers form the foundation for children's ability to experience and create positive relationships—in all forms. Within the relationship-based philosophy, teacher-child responsive interactions help infants and toddlers feel secure, safe, and less stressed. This frees children emotionally to love and learn.

# Creating a Relationship-Based Program

Close emotional relationships with infants and toddlers involve "caring for and caring about children; being available, attentive and perceptive; tuning in and following the child's lead; being supportive, but nonintrusive—allowing the child to exercise agency; sustained physical and perceptual presence; emotional availability and warmth and a deep knowledge of the child" (Eifer, 2006, quoted in Davis and Dunn, 2018).

A relationship-based program places the teacher-child, parent-child, peer, and teacher-family relationships at the top of the program's priority list. This type of program emphasizes children's sense of safety and security within caring teacher-child relationships. A relationship-based program places the needs of infants and toddlers for comfort, affection, protection, sensitive and responsive interactions, and warm, emotional connections as the primary priority. It emphasizes the importance of children's emotional and social development and ensures that teachers know how to help infants and toddlers feel loved and protected so that they will thrive physically, emotionally, socially, cognitively, and in language.

This type of program supports all domains of development within a play-based environment that recognizes children's need for self-initiated activities and the importance of guided teacher-child interactions that build children's sense of self-worth, curiosity, knowledge, skills, and desire to learn.

A relationship-based program supports and enhances quality parent-child relationships, knowing that children need and deserve to live in emotionally healthy environments at home and in programs. It creates a welcoming intake policy so that families feel secure in their choice of programs, and so that programs come to know children's interests, likes, dislikes, needs, strengths, and the families' goals for their children before they enter the program. For their well-being, emotional development, and learning, infants and toddlers need teachers and families to partner with each other.

A relationship-based program creates continuity of care where children stay with at least one of their teachers as the child progresses through the first three years. This type of program keeps groups of children together so that peers can bond and develop friendships. It provides a mentoring support system for teachers of infants and toddlers that emphasizes relationships among children, parents, teachers, and peers.

# Helping Children Feel a Sense of Belonging

A relationship-based program emphasizes meeting children's need to feel a sense of belonging. Feeling that you belong is feeling connected to others. Although it is not an emotion like happiness, sadness, fearfulness, or anger, we include it here because of its importance in the emotional life of infants and toddlers.

You develop an infant's or toddler's sense of belonging when you greet his family member at the door or when you smile and wave at the family if you are occupied with another child. A toddler who is not welcomed at the door with a big smile and a hello by a favorite adult may feel as if he does not belong in that learning environment. He stands at the door with his parent or family member, looking into the room, hesitant to enter. What he sees is a blur of people, colors, and shapes. How wonderful it would be if he saw the warm face of a favorite teacher and ran to her, deeply feeling her affection for him.

You develop children's sense of belonging when you:

- display photos of each child where the families of infants leave their child's coat or where a toddler leaves his favorite blanket for a soothing nap time.

- create an attractive bulletin board or group of pictures on the wall of each child's family and pets, displayed low enough so that infants in adult arms and toddlers can see them easily.

- provide laminated photos of families in a basket that infants can crawl to and explore and that toddlers can hold when they need comforting or want to show their family's pictures to a peer.

> "A sense of belonging is a human need, just like the need for food and shelter. Feeling that you belong is most important in seeing value in life and in coping with intensely painful emotions" (Hall, 2014).

- provide each infant the same crib each day and toddlers a mat or cot to nap on in the same familiar place each day.

- display children's scribbles and dabs of paint on a wall or bulletin board, with the child's name clearly written below the artwork.

- create a consistently familiar environment where a young infant can roll over on a safe floor mat, an older infant can crawl to find a favorite toy, a young toddler knows he can plop down and look at a book, or a two-year-old can find the crayons and paper.

- sing group songs, such as the following:

> *I have a friend, and her name is Sherry,*
> *I have a friend and her name is Sherry,*
> *I have a friend and her name is Sherry,*
> *Say hello to Sherry.* (everyone turns to Sherry and says, "Hi, Sherry")

- take photos of infants beside each other, young toddlers playing peekaboo, or older toddlers playing in the sand together and then create small books with these photos.

- look at the books with infants and toddlers or place them where infants and toddlers can enjoy them while snuggled together in a cozy corner.

- keep peers together if they transition to another room as they age.

You can also help young children feel a sense of belonging by encouraging them to interact with children with disabilities. Let a toddler feel helpful by asking her to turn on a faucet while you wash another child's hands. Encourage a child to bring toys to a child who has difficulty moving. The following wonderful interaction benefited both the child with disabilities and the other children without identified disabilities.

> Several toddlers sat by a child who had a challenging time moving. They looked into the child's eyes and imitated his sounds. The immobile toddler smiled and made more sounds. The interactive sound game continued for about ten minutes, much to the delight of everyone involved.

It may be surprising when peers consistently ignore or actively reject an infant or toddler. If children in your center or family child-care home push away or avoid a peer, observe carefully to determine when, where, and how the rejection occurs. If crawling infants move away from a certain peer, what behavior of that peer might cause other infants to avoid him? What behaviors do you observe in a toddler whom other children move away from when he moves through the room? Is there often a scowl on a toddler's face? Is the toddler whose peers reject him more likely to hit peers? Careful observation will help you know how to support a child who experiences rejection from peers.

## Recognizing that Infants and Toddlers Are Active Learners

Infants and toddlers are remarkable learners from the moment they are born. They are motivated to actively engage with you and the environment. They are thinkers and scientists. They must explore people, environments, and materials to learn. They have wonderful ideas about how the world works and are surprised when people or objects do something different than anticipated. For example, by eight months, infants expect that adults' emotional reactions will match whether the adult achieves a goal (happiness) or does not (sadness or anger) (Skerry and Spelke, 2014). They are surprised when adults' emotional expressions do not match the situation.

To learn about emotions, infants and toddlers must experience their own and others' emotional expressions. Young children must experiment with how their expression of emotions, such as distress, anger, and sadness, affects adults and peers. They need opportunities to see their expressions in a mirror. They need you to label these emotions, so they can learn their names. They need to hear stories from picture books about children experiencing different emotions. They need opportunities to hear you talk about those emotions. They must have opportunities to tell you about what they think a baby or little bear in a story might be feeling. Only then will they begin to learn the names of emotions and understand why a person might be happy, sad, afraid, or angry.

When you thoughtfully provide many opportunities to explore emotions, you are helping infants and toddlers understand how others feel and how to express their emotions in healthy ways.

# Setting Up a Responsive Curriculum

An infant and toddler curriculum is "everything that a child experiences each day" (Wittmer and Petersen, 2018). In a responsive curriculum, teachers observe individual children and provide interactions, activities, and environments that meet children's needs, interests, joys, and desire to learn. In a responsive curriculum, teachers use the following four strategies:

- Use the "serve and return" technique when interacting with children.
- Continually observe children's development in all domains and provide supports for that development.
- Set up challenging activities and interactions.
- Provide interactions and adaptations that are individually appropriate.

The "serve and return" technique involves observing children's cues, sounds, body movements, gestures, facial expressions, and words (children's serves) and returning with sensitive responses. These teacher responses generally result in turn-taking interactions between a teacher and child (Center on the Developing Child, 2020a).

Work as a team to continually observe children's development in all domains and provide materials, toys, interactions, and environmental creations, such as a pretend grocery store in the dramatic-play area, that support many children's ongoing development.

Set up activities and interactions that are challenging, age appropriate, and culturally respectful. Adjust the activities and interactions for each child's development level. Offer explorations such as mats of various levels for a newly crawling older infant or a storybook on dogs for a toddler with a new puppy (NAEYC, 2018).

Observe the strengths, joys, interests, and needs of each child—including children with identified disabilities—to provide interactions and environment adaptations that are individually appropriate.

# Developing an Emotionally Responsive Curriculum

In this type of curriculum, which emphasizes the emotional needs of children, the teacher-child relationship is a priority. Infants and toddlers need for you to be someone they can trust to care for them gently and lovingly and to value their emotions as real and important.

In an emotionally responsive curriculum, teachers use the following strategies:

- Focus on secure attachments between children and teachers.
- Constantly build on each moment to support children's emotional development.
- Observe individual children's emotional needs and strengths, and create environments and learning opportunities that meet those needs and strengths. For example, teachers plan opportunities for children to learn based on observations of the following:

  » The emotions that each child expresses and with whom
  » How each child expresses emotions
  » How each child shows that he is beginning to understand that others have emotions
  » How each child does or does not show compassion for others' distress
  » How each child manages his emotions; for example, how an infant becomes calm or a toddler learns to wait for a turn with a toy

- Consistently help children tell each other how they feel and respond to each other's feelings.
- Consider daily routines as valuable time to share emotions with infants and toddlers. For example, use feeding and diapering time as opportunities to connect with them.
- Use an emotionally based story form, such as the following, to plan their curriculum.

# An Emotionally Based Story Form

Child's Name: Akela     Child's Age: 5 months

Date: _____     Observer: _____

Today, Akela laughed for the first time in our program. Her teacher, Ally, put a toy pan on her head, and Akela thought that was very funny. Each time Ally took the pan off her head and then put it back on with a smile, Akela laughed. Akela and Ally played this game about 10 times before Akela became tired of it and stopped laughing.

**What is the child learning?**

Akela is learning how to take turns in a "conversation." She learned that when she laughs, Ally is likely to repeat the funny action. Akela experimented with a new way to express her emotions.

**What's next?**

- Read *Baby Faces* by Margaret Miller.
- Sing, "If You're Happy and You Know It" with Akela. Send home the words and actions to Akela's family.
- Continue playing surprise games that make Akela laugh.

**Ideas from Home**

(In this section, ask family members to share their ideas about Akela's laughter—when and where does she laugh? Ask if they have ideas about how to make Akela laugh.)

# Setting Up an Emotionally Rich Environment

In an emotionally enhanced environment, teachers think about how they can create safe and interesting spaces that encourage children's joyful and serious exploration and expression of emotions.

Consider the following strategies for creating an emotionally rich environment:

- Create learning areas in a room or family child-care program where infants and toddlers find comfort, safety, and warm teacher-child interactions.
- Create a cozy corner for one or two children, where older infants and toddlers can find quiet, softness, and beauty.
- Plan possibilities for emotional learning in each area of the room:

  » Posters with photos of children from diverse cultures and ethnic groups expressing a variety of emotions, such as anger, sadness, excitement, and happiness, placed low enough on a wall or end of a shelf so that infants and toddlers can see the pictures
  » Photos of the children in your program expressing different emotions
  » Culturally diverse puppets and dolls expressing different emotions, in a dramatic-play area
  » Puzzles depicting children's different emotions in a fine-motor or manipulative area
  » Storybooks (both purchased and created) that show children of different genders and from different cultures sharing and expressing many types of emotions
  » Storybooks in all areas of the room that show adults, children, and/or animals modeling emotional compassion
  » Playdough materials, such as cookie cutters, that express different emotions
  » Opportunities each day for older infants and toddlers to express themselves with art materials

- Provide equipment, toys, and materials that encourage cooperative peer play and learning:

  » Appropriate child-sized mats of various levels for infants
  » Slides, climbers, and blocks for toddlers
  » Cozy areas for two children
  » Several of each toy, so children can play together
  » An easel with two paintbrushes attached
  » Individual tubs with water, facing each other, so toddlers can play beside each other while talking and enjoying each other

# Using Emotional Activities Each Day

When you emphasize emotional development, children learn about emotions. In a study by Giménez-Dasí and colleagues (2015), researchers observed teachers who emphasized emotion knowledge, emotion regulation, and social competence in a program for six months. They found that the two-year-olds who participated in the emotion-promoting program gained more emotion knowledge than did a group who did not participate. Following are two examples of the activities that teachers used in this study.

**Looking for emotions: happiness.** In this game, the children are encouraged to find faces denoting a specific emotion—in this case happiness—on pictures found around the classroom. To do this, the teacher will have put images and photos all over the classroom expressing two emotions: happiness and sadness. The teacher will then ask the children to find the faces that are happy.

**The box of surprises.** This consists of a game of guessing the emotional expression hidden in the box. To do this, the teacher says the following rhyme:

*Happy or sad? How do they feel today?*
*You tell me, and we'll look right away.*

Then the teacher shows the children the hidden face for them to guess the emotion.

(Giménez-Dasí, Fernández-Sánchez, and Quintanilla, 2015).

Use the two activities described above in small informal groups with older toddlers. Informal groups are those that occur when a teacher announces an activity and many toddlers come running to see what is happening. Some toddlers who are engaged with other activities, such as the water table, may choose not to participate. The toddlers who do not take part in the informal group today will more than likely join in an interesting group activity tomorrow. It is perfectly okay when toddlers are fully engaged in other activities and do not want to participate in the informal group on a particular day. We want to promote and support toddlers' joyful engagement and attention span.

Other emotion-building activities include mirror activities, paper-plate faces, and dramatic play.

A mirror activity is wonderful for supporting young children's emotion knowledge. Several children can gaze in the mirror together. You can ask children to look happy, sad, surprised, fearful, or angry while looking in the mirror. You may have to model these faces and body movements for younger toddlers.

Use paper-plate faces in a variety of ways to enhance children's emotion knowledge. On paper plates, create a happy face on one side and a sad face on the other. You could also create paper-plate faces representing other emotions to use on another day. Glue the paper-plate faces to safe, toddler-appropriate sticks as handles. As you transition to go outside or wait for the food to arrive for lunch, give each child a paper-plate face. Ask the children how they are feeling. Have them look at the faces on both sides and ask them if they are feeling happy or sad. Ask them to show you how they are feeling. (They may need assistance. It is difficult for many toddlers to decenter and turn the side representing how they are feeling toward you.) You can ask each child to tell you how he is feeling and why.

Dramatic pretend-play games are another way for young children to explore and learn about emotions. Games where children step into a role, such as a firefighter, a store clerk, a mommy, or a daddy, can help them take the perspective of others and express emotions they otherwise may not feel comfortable showing. In fact, research shows that dramatic pretend-play games improve emotional control in four-year-olds (Goldstein and Lerner, 2018). Toddlers, too, practice emotional control when they pretend.

> Fergie, twenty-three months old, grabbed a doll in the dramatic-play area by the hair and dragged her across the room. She held up the doll and investigated her face. "You sad. You tired," she said to her doll. She put her in the doll bed on her tummy and covered her with a blanket. She plopped down beside the doll bed and

started to pat the doll's back and sing, "Tinkle tinkle, wittle tar." Fergie could not pronounce all the sounds, but she could carry a recognizable tune.

Fergie's emotion control grew during this activity. She had an opportunity to recognize the feelings of the doll. When she said, "You sad. You tired," she probably was expressing her own feelings. Fergie quietly sat by the doll bed. She had to control her arm movements and pat the doll gently, as a family member and a teacher had patted her in the past. She sang softly so that the doll could "go to sleep."

Older toddlers may pretend to be angry if the baby doll will not go to sleep. They express joy when you "eat" pretend food that they give you so generously. They often can hardly contain their excited emotions when you "drink" from a cup they have filled with pretend coffee.

Forms of dramatic play can occur at any time or in any place. For example, while waiting for a snack, you can ask toddlers to make a happy, sad, fearful, or angry face. Be sure to have them look at each other when they are making the faces. Take pictures and place them in a book that you make. Show them the book, and have them guess how the person in the picture feels.

# Building Relationships through Routines

Spend more time on routines; when we rush routines with infants and toddlers, they miss time to connect with you and their peers. Think of routines as one of the most important parts of your curriculum. Diapering and feeding infants are wonderful times for one-on-one interactions. Diapering and group eating times for toddlers offer many opportunities for "serve and return" conversations that build young children's strong and positive relationships with you and their peers, as well as build their communication skills. Notice how, in the following example, the teacher uses serve-and-return techniques to support both language and emotional development.

Naomi, a toddler teacher, invited twenty-seven-month-old Archie to the diaper table for a diaper change. Naomi encouraged Archie to climb up the steps to the table while holding on to her hand. She commented, "Archie, you walked *up* the steps." Archie smiled as Naomi encouraged him to help her pull down his jeans. In an encouraging voice, Naomi warmly stated, "Archie, you helped me pull off your jeans so we can change your diaper. Thank you." Archie again smiled as he sat down on the table and then lay down on his back.

Archie frowned and said, "Diaper owie." With a concerned look on her face, Naomi actively listened to Archie's expression of feelings and tried to figure out what Archie was trying to tell her.

Naomi said, "I think you are telling me that your diaper is hurting you. Let's take a look and see what hurts."

In this example, Naomi responds to Archie's movements walking up the steps with language. Archie served to Naomi with language when he said, "Diaper owie." Naomi returned his serve with language and a concerned look. She let Archie know that she heard what he was trying to tell her and that she would help him, both physically and emotionally.

Teachers holding young infants when they eat and sitting with toddlers when they sit at a table to eat are two especially important strategies for supporting all aspects of development, including emotional development. When teachers hold infants to feed them, they have opportunities to notice the children's facial expressions and match words to those expressions. They can acknowledge infants' likes and dislikes. They can respond to the infants' sounds as if they were conversational turns. When teachers sit with toddlers at a table, they can encourage children to talk about their likes and dislikes, animals that they have seen, how to help each other, or the colors of the food. You create a warm, caring atmosphere that nourishes both toddlers' bodies and emotional development.

# Reading Books and Singing Songs about Emotions

Many wonderful books and songs about emotions are available. The website Zero to Three (www.zerotothree. org) lists books for infants and toddlers "to help them navigate complex feelings and experiences, including anger, fear, grief and loss, and divorce." For example, for infants they suggest *Baby Faces* by Margaret Miller, and for toddlers they recommend *Lots of Feelings* by Shelly Rotner and *Grumpy Bird* by Jeremy Tankard. To help toddlers cope with anger, Zero to Three recommends books such as *Llama Llama Mad at Mama* by Anna Dewdney and many more. Many other websites list books for infants and toddlers about emotions, including Scholastic and Gryphon House. Always evaluate how you think a book will meet the needs of individual infants and toddlers.

Good books for infants include the following:

- Cloth books that are indestructible
- Books with large pictures and simple, bold images
- Books with a few words on each page
- Books with rhymes and rhythms
- Books with texture (fuzzy, rough, smooth) that infants can touch

Good books for toddlers include the following:

- Sturdy board books with large pictures and simple story lines
- Books that toddlers can handle often
- Books with rhymes and rhythms
- Books with texture (fuzzy, rough, smooth) that toddlers can touch
- Books with flaps that toddlers can lift to see new or surprising pictures

Start reading to infants as soon as they can focus on your face or a picture in a book. This means that you will start reading shortly after the infant is born. Read a book to an infant cuddled on your lap, so the child can hear your voice, see the pictures, and see you point to a picture as you talk about it. You do not need to read the book word by word. Watch the infant and see what interests him. If he is more interested in the pictures, then talk about them. Notice what he is looking at and talk about that. Give infants a chance to coo, babble, pat the book, and try to open pages. Babies will love books when together you create warm and responsive experiences during book-reading that build strong, caring relationships.

Toddlers may come running when you pull out a book. They will love to sit in your lap or remarkably close to you so they can see the pictures. Use your animated voice to capture the characters of people and animals and encourage toddlers' interest. Again, you do not need to read the book word for word. If that is boring to children, then tell a story about the pictures. Encourage toddlers to share their experiences with toys, babies, dogs, water, and other storybook topics. Reading to toddlers should be an engaging, interactive relationship-building experience.

Your singing can soothe a fussy baby, bring smiles to toddlers' faces, and actually help you experience positive feelings too. YouTube provides many examples of songs to sing to and with infants and toddlers. Songs about emotions are enhanced if toddlers can hold a paper-plate face expressing an emotion glued to the end of a toddler-safe stick. Puppets with smiling or grouchy faces engage toddlers as they sing about happy, sad, angry, and excited feelings.

# Encouraging Family Members to Read Storybooks about Emotions with Children

One of the most important things that families can do to support young children's language development and future reading skills is simply to read to them, beginning shortly after birth. Share the information in the previous section with families. Send home lists of appropriate books and reading tips for families of infants and toddlers, including the following.

- Start reading to infants shortly after birth.

- Read often, for short periods of time.

- Cuddle with infants as you show them the pictures in an infant book. Point to the picture and name it. Tell a brief story about the picture in an animated voice.

- Encourage toddlers to sit on your lap or near you so that they can see the pictures in a book.

- Do not expect toddlers to sit for a long time when you read a book. Capture their interest by reading a few pages and then encouraging the toddler to tell you about a picture or the content of the story.

- Even if the book is not specifically about emotions, comment on the facial expressions of the characters. Ask toddlers if a picture makes them feel happy or sad.

As you review a book for families to use with their children, think about the following:

- Does it accurately depict the facial expressions for different emotions?

- Does it talk about all emotions being legitimate and important?

- Does it demonstrate healthy ways for children to express anger, disgust, and sadness?

- Do the pictures represent several different ethnic groups?

# Creating Social-Emotional Activities for Adults

Create a social-emotional activity (SEA) for the week with your coteachers, families, and/or mentors. SEAs are social- and emotional-based activities for adults to use with children to gain knowledge about children's emotional growth and to support their emotional development. Following are seven examples.

- Use a variety of emotion words with the infants and toddlers in your group—not just *sad* and *happy*. Use words such as *frustrated, embarrassed, surprised, joyful*, and *disgusted*.

- Observe and chart for a week all the emotions that you see the infants and toddlers in your program expressing with their faces, gestures, and body postures.

- Chart all the emotion words that the toddlers in your program use during a week. If there are not any, then choose several emotion words to emphasize and model the next week.

- Take photos of children expressing different emotions, and create a book for the children. Ask family members to bring in photos of their children expressing different emotions.

- Ask family members to create a list of emotion words that their toddlers use at home.

- Create a poster of persons from different ethnic groups expressing emotions.

- Find two new storybooks that emphasize emotions. Read them to infants and toddlers, and place them in the storybook corner of the room.

# Summary

Use the following ideas from this chapter to create an emotionally responsive program for infants and toddlers.

- Work with coteachers to develop a responsive, relationship-based philosophy. Think about the most important behaviors and skills that you and families would like children to develop.

- Reflect on the key features of a relationship-based program. Consider each individual child and whether that child feels secure, safe, loved, and appreciated in your program.

- Consider whether each child feels a sense of belonging. Think about how to improve the program so that each child feels welcome, comfortable, safe, and excited about learning and relating to others.

- Reflect on how infants and toddlers in your program learn best. Observe them experimenting, exploring, and enthusiastically figuring out how toys, art materials, sand, water, and blocks work.

- Set up a responsive curriculum that builds on each child's interests, strengths, and needs.

- Develop an emotionally responsive curriculum.

- Set up an emotionally responsive environment that provides materials, such as dolls and puppets, that encourage emotional understanding and expression.

- Use emotional activities each day. Read books and sing songs about emotions.

- Use routines as a time to build relationships.

- Create an SEA for the week. These social-emotional activities help teachers to improve their practice in enhancing children's emotional development. For example, you could choose one strategy from this chapter, and focus on using that strategy for a week. Reflect on any changes that you see in yourself and the children.

- Encourage family members to read storybooks about emotions with their children.

# Key EIGHT

Learn Strategies to Support Children's Feelings and Temperaments

# Supporting Children's Unique Feelings

Infants and toddlers experience many different emotions. The emotions that they feel depend on their physical state, their experiences, and their temperament. They may feel affectionate one moment, then incredibly sad the next. Some children may bounce around and seem happy much of the time. Other children may frown and feel grouchy much of the time. Reading each child's emotions during each day requires your astute observation skills and your sensitive, responsive interactions. This approach will help children to grow and thrive emotionally with you.

## Children Who Feel Loved, Lovable, Affectionate, and Secure

If you want children to develop emotional competence, they must feel your deep affection for them and they must feel affection for you in return. Do you feel affection for the infants and toddlers in your program? If you do, you enjoy the children; show them that you really like them and want to be with them; are kind and compassionate with them; comment in a specific way on their positive and learning behaviors; welcome them and their families warmly in the morning; appreciate their struggles when they are learning to talk, walk, eat with utensils, use the toilet, and take turns with toys; comfort them when they feel distressed; and share your astute observations of their strengths and interests with their family members.

> Georgios, twenty-eight months old, ran to his favorite teacher. She bent down to see him better. He reached out his arms for a hug, and she hugged him. She said, "Good morning, Georgios. I'm so happy to see you." Georgios smiled a big smile and showed his affection by leaning into his teacher.

Do infants and toddlers in your program show affection for you as Georgios did in the example? If they do, they sometimes pat your back when you are holding them; put their hand on your cheek; wrap their arms around you; greet you with a smile in the morning; snuggle into you when you comfort them; crawl, toddle, or run to you when hurt; hug your legs; and enjoy spending time with you.

When infants and toddlers feel loved and can show love, they feel secure and safe. Their brains are not flooded with stress hormones. Instead, when they feel your affection, they can focus on building positive relationships and learning. Sometimes, teachers must work hard to interpret children's behavior as affection, as in the following example of Scout and her teacher.

> Twenty-five-month-old Scout tried to get her teacher's attention by patting her leg. When her teacher did not respond, Scout's pats became harder. The teacher looked down and in a warm, loving voice said, "Hello, Scout!" Scout smiled her biggest smile.

Toddlers often show affection to and seek affectionate responses from their teachers. They may give you toys, snuggle up to you, put their hands out for you to pick them up, try to talk to you, or, as Scout did, pat your leg too hard. They usually do not mean to hurt you. Instead, they are often seeking emotional closeness to you. When rejected, they may feel as if you do not care about them. If that happens often, then they may avoid you.

You may not feel the same amount of affection for all the children in your program. However, because you know that all children need affection, you show affection to all. Your lap is available, your voice is kind, and your compassionate eyes show all the babies and toddlers that you care when they look to you for reassurance, that they are people of value, and that you truly like them.

In the first three years of life, young children develop a sense of self-worth based on how others express emotions to them, and how others respond to their emotions. When they express emotions, they learn that someone either cares and responds or does not notice or care, that someone comforts them or scolds them, that someone pays attention or ignores them. The loving, emotion-facilitating experiences that infants and toddlers have with you and those who care about them are powerful influences on their healthy emotional development.

## Children Who Feel Happy, Joyful, or Gleeful

Most infants and toddlers who feel loved and safe are happy much of the time; they also can express their challenging emotions. Smile at infants and toddlers often to let them know that you are enjoying their company. Young children also try to make you laugh, as Emilio does in the following example.

> Being with you is what
> I call happiness.
>
> —Anonymous

When Emilio was four months old, he seemed to be making funny faces to make his teacher Gabriel laugh. By nine months, Emilio lifted his shirt to show Gabriel his navel. At fifteen months of age, Emilio began to offer a toy to Gabriel, but then pulled it back just as Gabriel reached for it. He laughed, and Gabriel joined in. By two years of age, Emilio pointed to his juice and with a sparkle in his eye he said, "Milk," and waited for the laughter from his teacher.

The joy for Emilio, as it is for almost all children, is in the responsive interactions with his teacher.

In one study, researchers found that toddlers were happiest when giving puppets a treat out of their own bowl of treats, rather than a treat that the researcher had just handed them. Taking a treat out of their own bowl meant that they had fewer to eat. These toddlers, under the age of two, were happier when they were sharing and being prosocial (Aknin, Hamlin, and Dunn, 2012). Adults can create opportunities for toddlers to give food or toys to others. For example, when a toddler needs a tissue, you can ask another toddler to take one to the child.

We hope that you see many smiles and hear many belly laughs, chuckles, and giggles in your program. If you are not seeing smiles or hearing laughter and giggles from yourself and the children, reflect on why happiness is not present in your room or program. Ask yourself the following questions:

- Do I smile often with the children?
- Am I sitting on the floor at their level so that I can really see when they enjoy an activity?
- Do I laugh with them when they laugh?
- Do I respond to their attempts to make me smile or laugh?

- Do I act surprised if they show me something interesting to them, such as a worm or the way a ball bounces?
- Do I set up a safe environment where peers can play games with each other, such as peekaboo or run and chase?

## Children Who Feel Sad, Despairing, Depressed, or Grief-Stricken

All infants and toddlers will feel sad at times. Infants who feel sad need adults who readily respond to their communication cues, greet them warmly, and smile at them frequently. When you see a toddler's quivering lips, watering eyes, or slumped shoulders, try not to talk her out of feeling sad. Instead, say, "We all feel sad sometimes. I wonder what is making you feel sad." You can offer children ideas for how to feel better after you have acknowledged their feelings.

Infants may be quiet, withdrawn, or smile infrequently when they are sad. If they are this way every day, they may be depressed. If you observe an infant who is frequently sad, help the family find services in the community that work with infants and their families together. You can find these services by searching online for "Infant Mental Health Services."

It may sound strange to say that sadness can contribute positively to a child's well-being and emotional health. Yet a child's sadness elicits care from adults when the child needs it. Also, a child's sad face demonstrates that she has empathy toward another who is sad, crying, or in despair (Lomas, 2018). The next chapter covers sad feelings that are more intense or challenging to infants and toddlers, such as despair, depression, and grief.

## Children Who Feel Curious, Confident, or Courageous

Most infants and toddlers are curious. They are always watching, listening, and learning. They then generalize about what they have experienced. If balls usually bounce, they expect all balls to bounce. If an adult gives them something that looks like a ball but does not bounce, they are intrigued and will try many times to bounce it. Next time you introduce a new toy or show children something outside, such as a caterpillar, look for the learning spark in their eyes.

Success creates children's sense of confidence. When you respond to an infant's cries in a nourishing way, the infant feels success at communicating his needs. When you create an environment that encourages toddlers' exploration, you are contributing to their sense of courage to venture away from you and interact with peers and materials. When you are the special person the exploring toddlers can return to when they are tired, hurt, or distressed, you are building their confidence and courage. This is because, when older infants and toddlers know that they have a trusted adult to return to, they are more likely to courageously explore an interesting but uncertain environment.

## Children Who Feel Fearful, Worried, or Anxious

Both infants and toddlers experience fear, worry, and anxiety. These feelings may come about because of past experiences but can also be a part of normal development. Many toddlers fear the dark, monsters, weather, strangers, separations, being alone, masks, or toilets (Ankrom, 2019). They also may have specific fears, such as bugs that fly, dogs of a certain color, or animals that slither. These more specific fears may develop because of frightening experiences. Toddlers also may model after an adult or peer who expresses a specific fear. If there is a child in your program who is particularly afraid of something or a situation, talk with the family to try to determine the cause or beginning of the fear. With the family, gently expose the toddler to what scares her; for example, show the toddler that there is a person under a Halloween mask. Read books about their fears—bugs, dogs, toilet learning. Most of all, understand that all toddlers have fears and need adults' sensitive help to manage these fears.

Fear and anxiety can be interrelated. Although they may produce similar responses, fear is the response to a known or observable threat; whereas, anxiety is the anticipation of an imagined or future threat (Ankrom, 2019). Most older infants and toddlers will feel anxious at times. They may look worried, look around fearfully, cling to an adult, or seem jumpy or tense. Infants and toddlers can feel vulnerable and often need protection. When you respond to their distress in a caring way, they become less stressed (Buss and Kiel, 2011).

Separation anxiety is one of the most common forms of anxiety for children and often occurs between eight and fourteen months of age (Bowlby, 1969). Older infants and toddlers become very clingy with their beloved caregivers and do not want the adults to leave them. They may cry and "fall apart." This type of anxiety occurs because of their new awareness that their favorite adult still exists when out of sight. This is called *person permanence* (Krøjgaard, 2005). Children's fear of strangers occurs around the same age.

As an infant and toddler teacher, you can help alleviate children's separation anxiety and stranger anxiety. When parents leave the room, encourage them to always say goodbye and be specific about when they will return (after lunch, after nap). When you leave the room, ensure that the child with separation or stranger anxiety is with another person she trusts. Then say goodbye and when you will return—even if it is for a few minutes. The smallest infant benefits when you respectfully tell him or her goodbye. When strangers enter the room, encourage them to talk with you first rather than with a child. If you smile at the stranger, an infant or toddler will often become less anxious.

Adults can encourage children who feel inhibited, anxious, shy, or withdrawn to gently try an unfamiliar activity. Researchers found that when parents gave no or little encouragement to shy toddlers approaching new situations, children's anxiety did not improve. Their anxiety also did not improve if parents pushed or strongly encouraged their children to take part in a new situation with new people. Toddlers' anxiety did improve if parents gently encouraged their children (Kiel et al., 2016). The following example shows how a teacher might gently encourage an anxious child.

DeAndre, twenty-two months old, hugged his teacher's legs when a stranger entered the room. DeAndre's wise teacher made eye contact with him and held his hand. The teacher asked DeAndre, "I am going to say hello to Alyssa's mother.

Will you come with me? I'll hold your hand the whole time." DeAndre held his teacher's hand tightly as they walked toward Alyssa's mom.

Another study concluded that toddlers are more likely to become anxious and withdrawn when adults punish them for feeling scared or frustrated (Engle and McElwain, 2011). The authors of the study found that this was true for boys more than girls. When scared or frustrated, infants and toddlers need your understanding. They need you to comfort them and verbally acknowledge their feelings, and with toddlers, to try to create mutually agreed-upon solutions.

Toddlers can feel anxiety that interferes with their everyday living. If you have a toddler who seems particularly anxious, talk with family members about your concerns. Give them ideas of ways to help, and implement more calming and comforting strategies in the program. If the anxiety does not improve, then discuss seeking added support from a community agency that evaluates children's development and provides infant mental-health services to the child, family, and program.

## Children Who Feel Angry or Frustrated

Anger or frustration is often children's response to adults, peers, or other triggers that prevent them from achieving a goal or cause them to feel restrained. Their faces show anger, they struggle or resist adults, and they cry or scream. Angry infants or toddlers may tense their bodies, arch their backs, and furrow their eyebrows. Toddlers may even throw themselves on the ground and flail around (Brooker et al., 2014).

An angry feeling serves a purpose for a child. A certain amount of anger may protect her from unnecessary and uncomfortable restrictions. For example, we have seen older infants who become quite angry if adults place them in an overstimulating restricted device, such as an activity center or bouncer that they cannot get out of by themselves. Anger and frustration also tell you that a child wants to pursue a goal. If anger and frustration levels are too low, infants may not pursue goals, such as making a toy piano play music. The child may give up on figuring out how a toy works. If anger is too high, it may interfere with goal attainment and end in frustration (Brooker et al., 2014).

Even two-month-old infants can become angry if their arms or legs are restricted (Izard, 1977). Infants' and toddlers' anger increases from four to sixteen months in most children (Braungart-Rieker, Hill-Soderlund, and Karrass, 2010) as they desire more freedom to explore, can tell you their wants and needs, and may need to be restricted for their own safety. Anger that is high much of the time may predict preschool behavior problems, especially if the child experiences high stress in his life (Brooker et al., 2014).

Infants and toddlers who are often angry or frustrated benefit from your understanding and warm-heartedness (Razza, Martin, and Brooks-Gunn, 2012). First, reduce a child's stress by building the child's secure attachment relationship with you (Brock and Kochanska, 2019). Responsiveness helps the child who is often angry or frustrated. When an infant wants out of a high chair, respond before he gets angry or frustrated, and thank him for letting you know he is ready to stop eating. This prevents the child's stress hormones from increasing. Model sign language for older infants and toddlers. This gives them a way to communicate their needs before they can say words and also when they struggle to use the few words they have. If you cannot respond quickly to help the child out of the high chair, then use your voice to soothe the child while she waits. When a toddler is playing with bubbles and does not want to stop to go outside, give her information as to when she will need to stop. Excitedly talk about all the adventures she will have when everyone goes outdoors.

See the next chapter for a more in-depth discussion about young children's anger, aggression, and defiance that interferes with a child's relationships.

## Children Who Feel Embarrassed, Ashamed, or Guilty

Embarrassment occurs when children are aware that others are evaluating their behavior. Toddlers become self-conscious. They realize that others are judging them. They may fear rejection if others disapprove of their behavior (Botto and Rochat, 2018). Try hard not to laugh at toddlers, but laugh with them when they laugh. Some become embarrassed, angry, and withdrawn when others laugh at them. Recognize that they care about what you think.

Earlier in this book we mentioned that there is a difference between guilt and shame. Toddlers who are shamed and embarrassed when they hurt others or damage objects are less likely to try to make amends than children who are given ideas or encouraged to think of ideas to make things right again (Drummond et al., 2017). Shaming includes saying things such as, "Don't be such a baby," or "Shame on you," or "You are a bad child." Shaming includes embarrassing a toddler in front of others. The toddler then focuses on her own feelings rather than the feelings of others.

# Supporting Children's Different Temperaments

Temperament describes the way that young children feel and think. Many researchers think that children are born with a behavioral style (Chen, 2018; Dollar and Buss, 2014; Krassner et al., 2017). Temperament influences children's mood, activity level, and how they interact with others. Some children seem positive while others seem more negative much of the time. Some children seem shy, and others seem friendly and outgoing. Some are calm, and others are excitable. A child might tend to be suspicious (of new foods, for example) or to frighten easily. Another child might dig right into a new food, excited about tasting it.

Infants and toddlers flourish when you understand that each one's temperament is different. You can respect those differences and work with them. Exuberant children may need your calming influence, and children who seem shy and withdraw from others will need your gentle encouragement to play with others (Grady and Callan,

2019; Kiel et al., 2016). Others will need more time to eat or try an unfamiliar activity. All children will benefit from your talking about their emotions (Grady et al., 2019).

Observe whether infants and toddlers react more intensely to voices, temperature, touching, and noise and seem bothered by them. For example, they may cry or become anxious if the noise level in the room increases or if other children are too close to them and invading their personal space. These children will need your sensitive skills of observing, understanding, and reacting in ways that support their ability to engage with others and learn.

# Involving Families to Better Understand Each Child

Partner with families to learn about each child's expression of emotions and temperament. Families can tell you when and why their children express different emotions. When you learn from a family, for example, about when and why a toddler becomes angry, you are more likely to be able to prevent the anger in your program.

Ask family members about their child's temperament and how you can better meet her needs. Share ideas with family members to support children who are frequently shy, outgoing, fearful, anxious, and so on, especially if these temperament traits are interfering with a child's ability to learn and interact successfully with others. If a family member shares that they are troubled by an infant who seems irritable at home, you can then brainstorm ideas with the family about how to support that child's temperament at home and in the program.

# Summary

Use the following ideas from this chapter to support infants' and toddlers' unique feelings and temperaments.

- Reflect on the many strategies that support children's unique feelings. There are different strategies for children who feel affectionate, happy, sad, confident, fearful, anxious, angry, embarrassed, ashamed, and guilty.

- Consider strategies that support children with different temperaments. You can observe each child's temperament, respect the differences in children's personalities, and use strategies that help them flourish.

- Involve families to better understand each child. Create opportunities to talk one-on-one with families.

# Key NINE

Understand the Different Types
of Emotional Stress

# In this chapter you will learn the following:

- The types of stress that young children experience

- Strategies to help you understand children's day-to-day positive and tolerable stress

- Strategies to support children who experience toxic stress, including adverse child events

- Strategies for children who feel socially stressed

- What to do when a child and family need intense therapy or intervention

We all experience stress in our lives. There are several types of stress that young children can feel and experience: positive, tolerable, toxic, and social stress. In this chapter, we will look at these types of stress and explore how to support young children who experience them. In particular, we will delve into the effects of toxic stress, including adverse child events, and the nourishing strategies that you can use to support children experiencing trauma. We will also consider what you can do when a child and/or family need more intense intervention.

# Understanding the Different Types of Stress

*Positive stress* is "a normal and essential part of healthy development" (Center on the Developing Child, 2020c). A child's heart rate may increase, for example, at his own special birthday party, or he might feel shy and uncomfortable about playing with a new group of children. If a caring adult is available to support the child, positive stress is beneficial for children as it encourages development, new experiences, and learning how to work through challenges.

*Tolerable stress* is "serious, temporary stress responses, buffered by supportive relationships" (Center on the Developing Child, 2020c). If a toddler falls and scrapes his knee, he experiences an increase in the fight-or-flight hormone cortisol. With supportive adult help, however, his stress levels will decrease over time. Both positive stress and tolerable stress—when buffered with supportive adult-child relationships—help children develop and learn healthy responses to stress (Center on the Developing Child, 2020c).

Children experience *toxic stress* when stress is extreme and long lasting, and the child does not have supportive, responsive relationships that buffer the stress. Toxic stress occurs when a child experiences *adverse child events*, a term used to describe events in a child's life that affect him in a harmful and negative way. This type of stress occurs when a child experiences grief, depression, neglect, abuse, exposure to violence, and punitive daily care. Infants and toddlers feel toxic stress when they witness family violence (Graham et al., 2015), even if a parent is not violent toward them. They experience toxic stress if they cannot predict what will happen to them, if their environment is chaotic, and if they are punished for behaviors beyond their control, such as being expected to use the toilet before they are physically able to do so.

The word *trauma* refers to the child's responses to toxic stress. When we say children have experienced trauma, we mean that they have experienced excessive and unhealthy emotional and physical stress. These children have experienced one event or ongoing events that overwhelm their stress system. Toxic stress interferes with a young child's brain development, emotion regulation, present and future physical health, and ability to form healthy relationships both now and in the child's future (Center on the Developing Child, 2020c).

*Social stress* is a term we use in this book to describe how children feel when they have a challenging time relating to their peers. They may use behaviors that hurt themselves and others or may withdraw from others in fear. Many of these children may be experiencing positive, tolerable, or toxic stress that affects how they interact effectively with others.

# Supporting Children Who Experience Positive and Tolerable Emotional Stress

Have you noticed that you may feel stressed even when you anticipate a positive event such as a vacation? This is true for young children as well. Even though something positive is happening for a child, such as Grandma coming to visit, infants and toddlers may feel the excitement but often do not fully understand what is causing the change in their feelings and those of others. They do not know what to do with the feelings of delight and anticipation. Stress, even positive stress, affects children's ability to manage their emotions. Infants and toddlers will need your constant understanding to observe their stress; provide your consistent day-to-day responsive, affectionate interactions; and help them with their feelings.

Remember that tolerable stress is temporary stress that adults buffer with their responsive attention (Center on the Developing Child, 2020c). For example, if a young child loses a pet, starts in a new program, or hurts himself on the playground, he will feel stressed. But with your responsive help, this type of stress will not become toxic to the child. Infants who feel temporary but confusing stress may be irritable, sleep, or cry more than usual, not eat well, and resist physical affection. Without caring adult help, toddlers may begin to use aggression, become more defiant, and become wary of people and their surroundings. At the end of a long day, an infant may become fussier and a toddler cry more easily, because children in programs and family child-care homes may become more stressed during the day (Bernard et al., 2015). However, a secure attachment with a teacher or home-care provider buffers this stress (Badanes, Dmitrieva, and Watamura, 2012). Developing secure attachments with infants and toddlers, embracing Care for the Spirit days, and creating a less stressful environment help to support children experiencing both positive and tolerable stress.

## Develop Secure Attachments with Infants and Toddlers

Creating warm, caring relationships with infants and toddlers is the most important thing that you can do to reduce their stress levels (Badanes et al., 2012; Lisonbee et al., 2008). If children have secure attachments to help offset their stresses, they can focus on loving themselves and others and on learning. The most effective ways to diminish stress levels in young children are to meet their needs for loving emotional connections, affection, and a sense of safety.

## Embrace Care for the Spirit Days

All children have days when they feel more emotionally challenged than usual. The reasons for a child's emotionally difficult day may include lack of sleep, hunger, illness, missing Mom or Dad, or troubles with peers. Infants' tummies may be upset. Toddlers may become dismayed, discouraged, and disheartened when adults intervene to keep them safe, just as they were having fun climbing on cupboards. These children need a Care for the Spirit Day (Colorado Office of Early Childhood, 2020; Wittmer and Honig, 2020).

> "The quality of teacher interactions is particularly crucial to decrease child stress. The nourishing adult makes sure each child is warmly welcomed and feels comfortable in the child-care setting. Particularly for infants and toddlers, freely available lap time is important. During the first weeks in care, cuddling and holding may be just what a baby needs to feel secure" (Honig, 2014).

A Care for the Spirit Day is one in which a child needs extra responsive attention from his special adults. You may need to hold a fussy infant more than usual. A toddler may need to sit in your lap or attach himself to you physically all day. Older infants and toddlers might try to follow you everywhere and cry when you leave the room. You will know that they are feeling emotionally fragile and vulnerable. Your kindness and understanding often is just what children need to fill their emotional cups. A Care for the Spirit Day may become a Care for the Spirit week or even month for some children. You may not know what caused the infant or toddler to need more of your affectionate care on certain days and weeks—you just know they need it! Please do not be concerned that you are giving them too much attention. Once their needs are fulfilled, infants' curiosity will blossom and toddlers' desire to explore and investigate their world will take over. These children will, however, always need your responsive, day-to-day, affectionate attention (Wittmer and Honig, 2020). Creating a less stressful environment in the program and talking with families may help you meet the needs of these children.

## Create a Less Stressful Ambiance

It is impossible to create a completely stressless environment; however, you can create an atmosphere in your room or child-care home that aims to reduce stress and thus provide a less stressful environment. Try the following strategies:

- Create a predictable environment. Infants and toddlers thrive when they can count on their favorite teachers being available each day and materials and equipment being in generally the same area each day. Chaotic environments add to children's stress levels. For example, dolls thrown into a basket together lead to children having difficulty finding the one they want. Dolls can be displayed on an easy-to-reach low shelf so that children can clearly see each one.

- Provide activity choices, and long periods of time to make choices, for infants and toddlers to support their active learning and self-initiation. Provide materials that are age, individually, and culturally appropriate (NAEYC, 2018), and offer safe water, sand, and creative experiences, such as crayons and paint, as choices to soothe children's stress.

- Evaluate how much softness you have in the environment. Add safe softness, such as pillows in the toddler reading area. Homelike environments with toddler-size couches help children's comfort level. Expose children to natural lighting as much as possible.

- Know that infants and toddlers can read your emotions. If you are stressed, they will be stressed too (Groeneveld et al., 2012).

- Engage in caring routines. Spend more time in one-on-one or small-group routines.

- Avoid hurrying infants and toddlers. Give infants lots of time to finish a bottle and toddlers lots of time to play, make choices, and clean up after play.

- Provide opportunities for outdoor play and experiences with nature.

- Recognize the value of quietly being present.

- Talk with families about how they reduce their children's stress levels.

# Understanding Children Who Experience Toxic Stress

When young children experience toxic stress, their bodies are consistently overwhelmed with stress hormones. These can negatively affect children's brain development and health and can have long-term effects. However, you and the other important adults in a child's life can make a positive difference. The Center on the Developing Child (2020b) emphasizes, "Stable, responsive, nurturing relationships in the earliest years can prevent or even reverse the damaging effects of early life stress, with lifelong benefits for learning, behavior, and health."

You may think that one person cannot make a difference in a child's life. Yet think about a supportive person in your life. What does that person do to help alleviate your stress? Your world is better because of that person. You can begin to believe in yourself again with that person. Research shows that for young children, having adults who believe in them—their capabilities, their strengths, and their positive attributes—makes all the difference in developing resiliency, the capacity to recover quickly from challenges (Weir, 2017).

Infants and toddlers need someone, or many people, who look beyond their crying, whining, disobedience, withdrawal, and aggression that they use to cope to see the child who is hurting and asking for your help. These young children experiencing toxic stress need as many adults as possible to see their potential, because they cannot voice their need for affection, unconditional love, and safe arms to hold them. In the following pages, we look more closely at how young children grieve, experience loss, and can feel depressed; how neglect and child abuse affect infants and toddlers; and what you can do to support these children who are trying to cope with many emotional challenges.

## Children Who Experience Grief, Loss, and Depression

Infants and toddlers grieve when they experience loss. Many people think that loss does not affect young children, but it does. If an infant suddenly loses his attachment figure, he may become sad and show signs of depression. He may stop eating, have difficulty sleeping, and refuse to let someone else comfort him. He may lose his enthusiasm for learning.

Toddlers become distressed and mourn when they experience loss of a favorite adult with whom they have developed a trusting, loving relationship. Toddlers, too, exhibit many of the same behaviors that infants do when they mourn. Toddlers also may start to express their emotions through aggressive behaviors, frequent crying, tantrums, or regression in abilities such as toilet learning. They may lack energy for everyday activities.

Many toddlers feel a loss when teachers move them too quickly to another room in a program and their beloved teacher stays behind. They lose the one who knows them best and understands their unique ways of communicating. They mourn the loss of their peers if teachers move them to a new room in a program without their group of friends (Wittmer and Clauson, 2018).

Infants and toddlers who experience the loss of a loved one may try to reject those who try to comfort them. They may attach themselves to any stranger who comes into their lives. This may seem like a healthy adaptation to their loss; however, this behavior reveals the deep need toddlers have for safety and attention. This behavior is concerning because the toddlers seek fleeting emotional experiences instead of experiencing deep and enduring relationships.

Following are some ideas of what to do if you know that infants or toddlers are grieving.

- Ensure that each child has someone who loves him dearly and is consistently emotionally available for him.

- Use continuity of care and group for all children so that they do not need to use unnecessary emotional energy to adapt to new teachers who will have unique ways of talking with them, new rules, and new environments. With continuity of care, at least one teacher stays with a group for their first three years in a program. With continuity of group, the program keeps groups of children together as they move to a new room in a program.

- Recognize that infants and toddlers grieve for extended periods of time. When adults say, "Oh, he's okay. He doesn't seem bothered. He's over it," they do not understand how infants and toddlers grieve. These children may at times be emotionally vulnerable, cry easily, and seek comfort and protection for years after an event, such as the death of a parent.

## Children Who Are Neglected

Severe neglect includes the ongoing disruption or significant absence of caregiver responsiveness. Johnson, Wilhelm, and Welch (2013) identified six types of child neglect.

### Table 9.1: Six Types of Child Neglect

| Type of Child Neglect | Definition |
|---|---|
| Physical | Adults do not meet the child's physical needs for food, shelter, clothing, and so on. |
| Medical | Adults fail to secure medical attention for the child. |
| Supervisory | The child experiences lack of adult supervision. |
| Environmental | The home of the child is filthy and/or dangerous. |
| Educational | The child lacks access to education. |

| Type of Child Neglect | Definition |
|---|---|
| Emotional | • Adults deprive the child of a positive, secure attachment with special adults.<br>• Adults reject or humiliate the child.<br>• The child receives bizarre punishments.<br>• The child is ignored continuously. |

Supervisory or emotional neglect in programs can occur when there are too many children and no individualized adult-child relationships that are reliably responsive (Center on the Developing Child, 2013). Neglect can lead to a child experiencing toxic stress. Significant child neglect can cause cognitive delays, impairments in attention and self-regulation of emotions and behavior, stunting of physical growth, and disruptions in the body's stress response (Center on the Developing Child, 2013).

# Children Who Experience Abuse and Trauma

Adverse child events include child abuse and other experiences of trauma, such as ongoing poverty, witnessing family violence, or loss of an attachment figure, causing the child to feel helpless and hopeless.

Child abuse may include physical abuse, sexual abuse, or emotional maltreatment. Infants under twelve months are most at risk of serious physical abuse (Davies et al., 2015). If you *suspect* that a child is experiencing abuse, you are legally required to report it to the proper state or county agency. Your program will have a policy for how to handle suspected child abuse. You may have an infant or toddler in your program who has experienced abuse and is now with a relative or in foster care. Children in your program who have experienced child abuse may exhibit the following behaviors:

- Have difficulty controlling their emotions
- Have activity levels that are higher or lower than other children
- Always seem to be on high alert and constantly worrying about doing something wrong
- Avoid or respond negatively to any kind of touch or physical contact
- Have a challenging time expressing their emotions without being aggressive or withdrawing

Trauma overwhelms the child's emotional system. The child is unable to make sense of events, such as seeing family violence or experiencing physical or sexual abuse, neglect, the death of a sibling, a serious illness, natural or human caused disasters, or separation from loved ones (Center for Early Childhood Mental Health Consultation, 2008). Infants and toddlers who experience trauma may:

- have eating and sleeping disturbances;
- have new and more extreme fears;
- startle easily;
- experience delayed development, including emotional, social, cognitive, language, and motor development;

- often become angry, aggressive, or clingy;
- have difficulty complying with directions and requests; and
- act out their traumatic experiences during play, such as repeatedly hitting a doll.

Toxic stress response also can occur when a child experiences caregiver substance abuse or mental illness, exposure to violence, and/or the accumulated burdens of family economic hardship—without adequate adult support (Center on the Developing Child, 2020c).

## Strategies to Support Children Who Experience Toxic Stress

We want infants and toddlers to grow toward emotional competence. Review Table 2.1 on pages 11–13 and think about the aspects of emotional competence you want the children in your care to develop.

- Never assume that a child is purposely not listening or is aggressive because he wants to be. Look beyond the behavior to the child who is trying so hard to cope and manage his personal and physical environments.

- Always try to consider how children are feeling and what may be causing them to experience behavior that is challenging to themselves and others. You are the detective. With your team and the children's families, learn about the factors in the child's life that are contributing to the behavior.

- Look for the child's unmet needs. These include the child's needs for secure attachments, safety, healthy food, exercise, love, positive attention, caring relationships, and opportunities to learn. Try to provide, along with the family, for these unmet needs.

- Use active listening strategies. This is one of the most important strategies that you can use to support young children's emotional development. Always try to use this strategy first before using other strategies. When you use this strategy, you are becoming in tune with the child. When you comment on what you think the child is feeling you are using mind-mindedness strategies. You are trying to read the mind of an infant or toddler who has difficulty telling you exactly how he is feeling. When you say to an infant, "I hear you. Are you hungry? It is hard to wait, isn't it?" in a soothing voice, you are actively listening. You are using active listening when you say to a toddler who has fallen to the floor in anguish because he cannot go outside, "It is so hard to wait to go outside. I understand your feelings. You really want to go outside now. You can tell me, 'I'm really frustrated.'" You are not only helping infants and toddlers identify their challenging feelings but also letting them you know you understand and will help them.

- Be physically and emotionally available to children. They must learn to trust special adults in their lives and believe that caring relationships are important.

- Respond promptly to children's cries of distress. When children get too upset, their brains flood with toxic stress chemicals (Narvaez and Witherington, 2018). Nurture children who feel distressed by helping them become calm when they feel overwhelmed (Imrisek, Castaño, and Bernard, 2018).

- Spend one-on-one time as often as possible to engage in "serve and return" communication exchanges. These help infants and toddlers feel what communication is like and learn how to interact in satisfying ways with others.

- Create an environment to encourage engaged play. In an environment created for children to play in, they can experiment with toys and materials in ways that allow them to be successful (Sciaraffa, Zeanah, and Zeanah, 2018). When infants and toddlers experiment and figure out how to make a car roll or toy bus doors open, they begin to believe in their capabilities to solve problems. They feel the satisfaction of accomplishing a task. Be sure to offer interesting materials that children at different developmental levels can use successfully. For example, an infant can enjoy baby rattles. A young toddler can place the same rattles in containers and shake them to make unique sounds. Older toddlers can use them in dramatic play as they play with dolls and as they pretend to be babies themselves. As children play, we hope that they will look to you to enjoy their success with them.

- Encourage children in specific ways, such as saying in an approving and enthusiastic voice, "You used six blocks to build your tower. You worked hard." The child feels noticed, appreciated, and admired, which leads to a sense of self-worth. He learns that his effort, not just the outcome, is what is important. This leads to a willingness to try, even though he knows that sometimes he will fail.

- Notice and encourage prosocial behaviors, such as helping, showing kindness, and giving. Say, "You are a person who likes to help others." This type of comment helps the child view himself as having this characteristic.

- Give choices to toddlers, either verbally or nonverbally by pointing. Say, "Do you want to build with blocks or paint?" These types of questions build toddlers' sense of autonomy—a feeling that they can make good decisions—and give them a sense of control.

- Teach problem-solving skills to toddlers when there is a conflict. Ask, for example, "Do you want to ask Summer for the toy or wait here by me until she finishes?" Problem-solving skills are life skills that lead to healthy relationships with others as well as contributing to children's belief in their own competence.

- Work closely with the child's family or the foster family to meet the emotional needs of the child.

- Work closely with community agencies that have services to support you, the child, and the family.

# Supporting Children Who Experience Social Stress

Most young children will need your encouraging support to engage with peers in helpful, kind, and problem-solving ways. Some children, however, will need additional thoughtful, understanding, and supportive strategies to learn how to manage their emotions. Those children who hurt others and those who withdraw from their peers are feeling socially stressed. You can help by meeting their needs and teaching them more prosocial strategies so that they enjoy their peers.

## Children Who Hurt Others

Aggressive behaviors such as hitting, biting, grabbing toys, pinching, kicking, or slapping adults and peers increase in frequency between twelve months and three years of age (Alink et al., 2006). This increase in aggression occurs in many cultures and countries. With adult support, however, most children learn strategies to manage their emotions in healthy ways. Following are some ideas for what to do if an older infant or toddler uses aggression often in your program.

- For a child who often hurts others, start his day by connecting emotionally with him. Greet him at the door. Let him know how happy you are that he is here today. Comment positively on something that the child did yesterday. Say, for example, "I'm so glad to see you. Do you want a hug? Do you remember yesterday when you helped Angus when he cried? You took a blanket to him. That made him feel so good. You are a helper."

- Phrase directions in a positive way. Say, "Pat gently," as an older infant or toddler pats another child.

- Notice many of the kind, loving, affectionate, helping behaviors of older infants and toddlers. Comment on these behaviors. Say, for example, "I saw you give a toy to Enola. Thank you, Enola liked that. See her face. She is smiling."

- Do not match toddlers' anger with yours. Your anger contributes to increased toddler anger.

- React with a firm but calm voice to a toddler who has just hit or bitten or grabbed a toy from another toddler. Explain how this behavior hurts the other child or how the other child might feel.

Use the ABCDR approach to guidance (Wittmer, 2020). For example, you see LeBron hit Matias. You do not know what happened prior to the hit. Put yourself at the child's eye level and speak in a sincere voice using words appropriate for that child's development level:

**A: Acknowledge feelings, use Active listening, show Affection and Appreciation** to both children's feelings and intentions. Depending on the child's developmental level, you can say, for example:

"Tell me what happened."

"LeBron, you did not want him to take your truck."

"Matias, you wanted the truck. You both want the truck."

Often, toddlers cannot tell you how they feel. You can make wise guesses as to their feelings and intentions.

**B: Behavior (present and future) and Brainstorm:**

*Present Behavior*: Say, "You both want the truck. You felt sad (frustrated, angry). I saw you hit Matias. No hitting others. Hitting hurts. Use your words or tell a teacher."

*Future Behavior*: Ask yourself what behavior you want the children to learn to use in the future during conflict. Offer these suggestions to the children, such as the following:

- Using words or sign language instead of hitting
- Asking the teacher for help
- Taking turns
- Getting another toy

You want them to show empathy, care for each other, like each other, and play well together.

Brainstorm if children are able. Ask, "What can we do to solve the problem?" If children cannot think of solutions, suggest two solutions that are appropriate to the children's developmental level, such as the following:

- "You could play with the truck together."
- "Matias, you see the blue truck over on the floor? You could get that one, and you and LeBron could play together."

- "Matias, you could ask LeBron for the truck. Let's practice. Say, 'Can I play with the truck?' "If LeBron says no, then give Matias some alternatives to encourage his self-regulation: "Matias, you could wait here patiently on the floor or go get that blue truck over there [pointing]. You could ask LeBron to tell you when he is finished."
- "LeBron, you could say to Matias, 'I need my truck right now. I will share soon.' Let's practice."

**C: Care:** Show you care for each child. Each time a conflict happens, emphasize how to care for each other. You could say, for example, "We care for each other here. We want to keep you and others safe. We are learning to be kind to our friends."

Continually help toddlers think about how others are feeling and encourage them to help each other. If a toddler is crying, take another toddler along to soothe the crying child. Encourage the noncrying toddler to think of ways to comfort the crying toddler. Increased empathy is related to decreased aggression (Noten et al., 2019).

**D: Deliberate Thinking:** Step back, and with your team, supervisor, or mentor, think about what may be causing the behavior—in this case a conflict over toys. What are the needs of the children? What may be causing the behavior? For example, are there enough toys in the environment? Examine your environment and

schedule. Is the schedule relaxed? If teachers hurry toddlers from one activity to another, toddlers may become aggressive. Do you allow individual children to make choices within a thoughtfully arranged environment full of many learning opportunities? If teachers herd toddlers together in a group from one learning center to another rather than allowing individual children to choose, they will be stressed. Arrange the environment so that toddlers easily can see learning centers for blocks, manipulatives, large-motor play, reading stories, and art. This allows them to choose their activities and become engaged for extended periods of time. A chaotic environment can lead to aggressive toddler behavior.

**R: Relationships:** Create a relationship-based environment and ambiance in your room or family child-care home. After a conflict or aggression between children, restore relationships. For example, you could ask LeBron and Matias to help you carry a bucket of water to the water table. Both children will need to cooperate to carry the bucket, and they will have fun together.

Give information to families on positive guidance. Families who use physical punishment and belittling discipline techniques are more likely to have children who are more aggressive (Benzies, Keown, and Magill-Evans, 2009). The National Association for the Education of Young Children (www.naeyc.org) has many free publications for families on a wide variety of topics, including positive guidance. You can order brochures to give to families or download short articles for them. Zero to Three (www.zerotothree.org) also has many easy-to-read articles and brochures on topics that interest families.

A small number of children angrily bite and hit others beginning at six months of age (Hay et al., 2014). These children and their families need immediate emotional support and intervention provided by your program or a community mental health agency. A family may be experiencing stress, have a child with a temperament that is challenging them, or need support to feel positive about their child.

# Children Who Withdraw

You will notice some older infants and toddlers who seem fearful of others. They withdraw, often do not want peers near them, and react with tears or aggression if other children invade their space. These children may have a shy temperament, experience sensory challenges, or are fearful. They need adult support to enjoy others and learn to play with peers. Teachers and parents will need to adjust their social expectations for children who are shy. Research has shown that children who are shy benefit from adults who gently encourage them to engage with others but do not force them to do so (Rubin et al., 2002). Following are some strategies to use with children who withdraw.

- Put on your detective hat, observe, and make wise guesses as to why a child might withdraw. Only then will you be able to find solutions.

- If the child experiences sensory challenges with touch or too much stimulation, try to make accommodations for him. For example, some children become overwhelmed when there is too much noise or many types of noises. After observing this, you can help this child avoid loud noises.

- If the child is shy or fearful, increase his trust in his special adults by being emotionally and physically available. Work on adult-child relationships before peer relationships.

- Once the child seems securely attached to his special adults, begin to include another child when you read a book or engage in an activity with the child who withdraws.

- Go with the child to play with others outside on a toddler slide or to kick a ball with a small group.

- Encourage a toddler who is socially adept to invite the toddler who withdraws to join her in a cozy corner.

- Take two children to investigate a mirror together, touch their noses in the mirror, and laugh at the funny faces they make.

- Sit the toddler who withdraws by a toddler who is very friendly for snack or lunch.

# When a Child and Family Need Intensive Support

Many factors influence the quality of a child's and family's life. These factors include parents' and children's health, family income and housing, and the type and amount of support the family receives. Families benefit from four distinct types of support—emotional, physical, material/instrumental, and informational (Kyzar et al., 2012). When any of these types of support is missing, families may have difficulty meeting infants' and toddlers' emotional needs (Zeng et al., 2020).

You and your program provide families emotional, physical, and information support. You provide emotional support when you listen to a parent's concerns and share positive information about his child. You provide physical support by providing a safe, quality care-and-learning program where infants and toddlers are learning to understand and express emotions in relationship-based ways. You provide informational support when you share websites, YouTube videos, brochures, and bulletin boards on positive guidance and parenting strategies.

You provide trauma-informed care for infants and toddlers when you create a cozy, calm, and interesting environment and emphasize the importance of teacher-child relationships. You support infants and toddlers who are experiencing or have experienced trauma when you focus on supporting their self-regulation through your willingness to comfort them in distress and support their sense of self-worth and problem-solving abilities

(Duke University, Sanford School of Public Policy, Center for Child and Family Policy, 2020). You are meeting the needs of young children who experience trauma when you look beyond the behavior of a child to discover the needs of that child.

Some families, however, will need additional support. Families of children who experience increased aggression, sadness and depression, grief, neglect, child abuse, trauma, and toxic stress often need intense help from community mental-health agencies. Families and children who have experienced trauma may benefit from trauma-informed care (Kistin, 2014). This type of intervention for parents considers how a parent's earlier trauma impacts how they parent and how they feel about parenting. Work with your program director to learn how to refer a family and child for intervention services.

There are highly effective interventions that support children with emotional challenges and their families. These interventions often also support the child and teachers in the program the child attends. One example of an intervention program that is effective with parents of toddlers experiencing emotional challenges is *Tuning in to Toddlers*. It is an emotion socialization program for parents of toddlers (Havighurst et al., 2019). The program improves parents' emotional responsiveness and emotion coaching to support toddlers' emotional development and prevent social and behavioral challenges.

Do not delay when you think that an infant or toddler is more depressed, sad, angry, or aggressive than you typically see in most children. It is critically important for the child and family to receive help in the first three years of life.

# Summary

Use the following ideas from this chapter to support infants and toddlers who feel challenged emotionally.

- Share the information on the three types of stress with coworkers and families.

  » Positive stress is a type of stress that is a normal and essential part of healthy development.

  » Tolerable stress is a serious, temporary stress response, buffered by supportive relationships (Center on the Developing Child, 2020c).

  » Toxic stress is extreme and long lasting, and the child does not have the supportive, responsive relationships that buffer the stress.

- Use strategies that reduce children's tolerable distress before it becomes toxic stress. Think about each child's experience and whether each child feels securely and affectionately attached to at least one adult in your program.

» Embrace Care for the Spirit Days when a child or children need added affection, soothing, and to be near you.

» Review your environment and reflect on how you can create a less stressful atmosphere.

• Children who experience toxic stress include those experiencing grief, neglect, child abuse, or ongoing environmental stress. Know that children experiencing toxic stress will have a challenging time managing their emotions.

» Look beyond the behavior to a child who is hurting emotionally and has great unmet needs.

» Respond quickly and warmly to children who feel distressed before stress hormones flood their brains.

» Choose strategies listed in this chapter to try to support children who feel challenged emotionally.

» Social stress can have a significant effect on children.

» Learn your program's policy concerning working with families when you, with coworkers, think that a family and child may need more intensive intervention than you can provide.

» Reflect on how your relationship-based program can provide continuity of care and move groups of children together.

» Provide additional support and relationship-centered solutions for children experiencing social stress—children who feel challenged with social experiences with peers.

# Key
## TEN

Know and Appreciate Your Importance

## In this chapter you will learn the following:

- The importance of developing caring relationships with infants and toddlers as an important, powerful, and influential part of your profession

- Strategies to create trusting relationships with families for the children's benefit

- How to partner with families to support children's emotional development

- The importance of recognizing children's influence on you

- Strategies to manage your feelings with children

- The importance of finding a coach or mentor who is emotionally available to you

- What to do when you are feeling stressed

- The importance of you

The infant and toddler caregiving profession is one of the most rewarding and most challenging of all professions. This career requires that teachers develop warm, caring, and loving relationships with children. Young children must feel cherished, admired, safe, and secure in order to thrive. Your profession requires that you develop close and trusting relationships with children and families. Most professions do not demand the same level of compassion and affection for the people served by them.

# Appreciating the Significance of Caring Relationships

You are an incredibly important person in young children's lives. Your mutually caring relationships with the infants and toddlers you spend time with each day influence whether they thrive or not. You will know if an infant feels safe with you if she nestles into you and you can easily calm her crying. You will know if a toddler genuinely likes you if she greets you with a smile, wants to be near you many times during a day, and quickly scampers close to you for emotional refueling. These infants and toddlers quickly learn whether they can trust you to meet their needs and whether they enjoy and feel secure with you. The caring relationships that you experience with infants and toddlers build their sense of well-being, which will affect them now and in the future. The feelings of self-worth that you help them develop become a part of who they are and influence how they love and learn. You are important in infants' and toddlers' lives.

# Creating Trusting Relationships with Families to Support the Children and You

You understand that creating trusting relationships with families is important for young children's sense of well-being and emotional development. A positive relationship between teachers and families eases families' concerns and makes your job easier and much more emotionally satisfying. Listening to families' hopes, dreams, wishes, and concerns about their children is a first step toward developing trusting relationships with family members. Another way is to share positive stories with them. When you share the good times in your program, family members feel positive about their child and you.

> When Sam, twenty-three months old, bit Carlos on the arm (without breaking the skin), Carlos went running to the teacher. He held up his arm for her to see and said, "Sam bite." Before his teacher could say or do anything, Carlos ran back to Sam and exclaimed, "No bite, friend." When the teacher told this story to Carlos's grandmother at the end of the day, his grandmother beamed with pride.

Because you share good times, you develop positive relationships with families that allow you to share information that may be more difficult to communicate.

Express to parents that you recognize parenting is not easy. That is why it is important for you and family members to cherish and focus on the positive moments. *Relational savoring* is the term used by Burkhart et al. (2015) to describe cherishing or prolonging the emotions associated with positive events and bonding experiences between the parent and child. In one study about this topic, researchers encouraged a group of parents to embrace relational savoring in their interactions with their children. Another group of parents was encouraged to savor their own individual experiences rather than relationship experiences with their children. After two years, those parents who used relational-savoring techniques reported more feelings of closeness with their children than did parents who were told to savor their own individual experiences (Burkhart et al., 2015).

# Partnering with Families to Help You Support Infants' and Toddlers' Emotional Development

Partnering with families to support children's emotional development helps you, children, and families. Children are happier and less stressed when teachers and families emotionally connect to form an alliance for children's benefit. When you and families work closely together to build infants' and toddlers' emotional competence, everyone thrives. Your job becomes easier when both you and families emphasize children's emotional competence at home and in your program.

Model for families the following emotion-building strategies with children in the program. Also, share them with family members through texts, bulletin boards, newsletters, special notes, posters with pictures, and when discussing emotional development of the children with their family members.

- Share information about how important it is for young children to gain emotional knowledge. For infants and toddlers to gain emotional knowledge, adults must talk often about emotions—both children's and their own.

- Share information about the importance of not minimizing children's emotions, but instead using words to describe children's emotions (Ornaghi et al., 2019).

- Encourage families to use emotional coaching strategies, such as encouraging their children to describe how they are feeling (Lauw et al., 2014).

# Recognizing Children's Influence on You

Each child's unique personality, how she communicates with you, her social competence, how much she cries or feels distressed, and her responsiveness to your care and interactions influence you each moment. For example, Vallotton (2009) found that how much and well an infant communicates with a teacher predicts a teacher's responsiveness. Infants, even those as young as two months, who communicate their needs more clearly with gestures, body movements, and sounds receive more responsive attention from adults. An infant who has more difficulty communicating is less likely to receive the attention that she needs. A reflective practitioner constantly examines how an infant's behavior influences how she interacts with that child.

In another study, researchers found that teachers of preschool children who were less aware of how they (the teachers) were feeling tended to ignore, minimize, or punish children's expression of feelings (Denham, Bassett, and Zinsser, 2012). A thoughtful teacher is aware of her feelings toward each child and talks with others to figure out how to interact with children who ignore or challenge her.

## Managing Your Feelings with Children

Infants and toddlers are watching and listening to you. They are also imitating you. These young children are learning from you how to manage their difficult feelings. If you stay calm when they feel distressed, and you comfort them and help them focus on how they can become happy or satisfied again, they will learn from you. If you express your distress with a toddler who bites another toddler without becoming angry or punishing, children will learn from you. If adults lose their tempers with children, angrily punish children rather than teaching them positive behaviors, and frown and scold children, they cannot expect infants and toddlers to learn to manage their emotions in healthy ways. You are always on stage with young children watching, listening, and learning from you.

It is easy, however, to feel challenged when you are in this role. What happens, for example, if a baby's crying makes you feel grouchy and angry? It can be frustrating to try to help a baby who is not responding to your caring techniques for soothing an upset infant. Reframing is a technique that some adults use to help manage their upset feelings. For example, when therapists helped parents understand that their infants' crying was a way of communicating distress (reframing)—and not a means to punish the parents—they were better able to help the infant (Riem and Karreman, 2019).

Mind-mindedness is another useful technique to calm your distressed feelings. Stop and try to put yourself in the mind of the child. What is the child feeling? What does the child need? A crying child may be feeling pain. The child may not know how to calm herself. A crying child may not know what she wants and needs. When all else fails, brainstorming different ideas with coteachers and being kind and understanding helps children most.

## Finding a Coach or Mentor Who is Emotionally Available to You

Working with infants and toddlers is one of the most important professions, but it can also be highly stressful. Researchers have found that when infant and toddler teachers receive an opportunity to create a relationship with an emotionally available coach, they are able to develop more positive relationships with the children in their program than did those teachers who did not receive coaching (Biringen et al., 2012). You will benefit from a coach who understands the challenges of your job and focuses on the positive things that you do.

It is helpful to have someone you trust to help you reflect on children's behavior and family concerns. Ideally, you would find a mentor or coach who listens to you, problem-solves solutions with you, and with whom you can develop a close relationship. You may find such a person in a local child-care and referral agency in your community or within your professional network.

# Knowing What to Do When You Are Feeling Stressed

Your stress levels influence how you respond to infants' and toddlers' needs. If you are stressed, tense, worried, and anxious, you may at times be emotionally unavailable to them. When you have your own emotional challenges, it can be difficult to enjoy your job and to remember how important each moment and day is to a child. Your life circumstances, such as your own family concerns, can interfere with your ability to focus on and cherish your work. Unless you are an expert at blocking out family concerns, it is only normal to bring those worries to work.

Added to that is the stress of the work with infants and toddlers. It requires a great deal of energy to care for children and develop loving relationships with them. It may be hard to convince others that loving children is a crucial part of your profession.

When you are feeling stressed, you can remind yourself of the importance of your work with infants and toddlers. With your coworkers, learn stress-reduction strategies such as breathing, reflection, and meditation. Toddlers will love to practice some of these techniques with you.

# Recognizing the Importance of You!

We end where we began—honoring the importance of caregivers in infants' and toddlers' lives. You make a difference in how young children feel about themselves and others. You recognize young children's emotional talents for relating with others— their emotional capital. You strive alongside families to support children's growth toward emotional competence. You set the stage for emotional learning and encourage children to become players with you on that stage. You use responsive, relationship-based strategies when interacting with children and when designing the curriculum. You thoughtfully manage your own emotions so that you are a model for infants and toddlers.

> "Maybe we need to flip a switch in our minds and realize that taking care of a child is arguably the most important and challenging job in the world" (Harari, 2018).

We hope that you recognize your own importance in developing infants' and toddlers' emotional well-being. Along with families, you hold the emotional future of young children in your hands. Be present, emotionally available, and emotionally skilled with these young children whom you are empowering to become emotionally competent.

# Summary

Use the following ideas from this chapter to support infants' and toddlers' emotional development and your own knowledge of how important you are in the lives of young children and their families.

- Appreciate that infant and toddler professionals develop caring relationships with young children because that is what these children deeply need to thrive.

- Review the importance of creating trusting relationships with families for the children's benefit as well as yours.

- Share information with families concerning the importance of emotional development and strategies to support this critically important aspect of a child's growth.

- Reflect with coworkers concerning children's effect on you.

- Consider how you manage your feelings with children. Are there children who are more likely to make you feel sad, frustrated, or angry? If so, reflect with coworkers on strategies to manage your legitimate feelings.

- Find a coach or mentor who is emotionally available to you.

- Recognize your stress and find ways—individually and with coworkers—to manage it.

- Recognize and appreciate the importance of you!

# References and Recommended Readings

Addyman, Caspar, and Ishbel Addyman. 2013. "The Science of Baby Laughter." *Comedy Studies* 4(2): 143–153.

Aknin, Lara, J. Kiley Hamlin, and Elizabeth Dunn. 2012. "Giving Leads to Happiness in Young Children." *PLoS|ONE* 7(6): e39211.

Alink, Lenneke, et al. 2006. "The Early Childhood Aggression Curve: Development of Physical Aggression in 10- to 50-Month-Old Children." *Child Development* 77(4): 954–966.

Alvestad, Torgeir, et al. 2014. "Challenges and Dilemmas Expressed by Teachers Working in Toddler Groups in the Nordic Countries." *Early Child Development and Care* 184(5): 671–688.

Ankrom, Sheryl. 2019. "The Difference between Fear and Anxiety." Verywell Mind. https://www.verywellmind.com/fear-and-anxiety-differences-and-similarities-2584399

Ardiel, Evan, and Catharine Rankin. 2010. "The Importance of Touch in Development." *Paediatric Child Health* 15(3): 153–156.

Badanes, Lisa, Julia Dmitrieva, and Sarah Enos Watamura. 2012. "Understanding Cortisol Reactivity across the Day at Child Care: The Potential Buffering Role of Secure Attachments to Caregivers." *Early Childhood Research Quarterly* 27(1): 156–165.

Basilio, Marisol, and Cintia Rodriguez. 2017. "How Toddlers Think with Their Hands: Social and Private Gestures as Evidence of Cognitive Self-Regulation in Guided Play with Objects." *Early Child Development Care* 187(12): 1971–1986.

Belacchi, Carmen, and Eleonora Farina. 2012. "Feeling and Thinking of Others: Affective and Cognitive Empathy and Emotion Comprehension in Prosocial/Hostile Preschoolers." *Aggressive Behavior* 38(2): 150–165.

Benzies, Karen, Leslie-Anne Keown, and Joyce Magill-Evans. 2009. "Immediate and Sustained Effects of Parenting on Physical Aggression in Canadian Children Aged 6 Years and Younger." *Canadian Journal of Psychiatry* 54(1): 55–64.

Bergland, Christopher. 2015. "How Do Various Cortisol Levels Impact Cognitive Functioning?" *Psychology Today*. https://www.psychologytoday.com/us/blog/the-athletes-way/201506/how-do-various-cortisol-levels-impact-cognitive-functioning

Bernard, Kristin, et al. 2015. "Examining Change in Cortisol Patterns during the 10-Week Transition to a New Child-Care Setting." *Child Development* 86(2): 456–471.

Białecka-Pikul, Marta, 2018. "Waiting for a Treat: Studying Behaviors Related to Self-Regulation in 18- and 24-Month-Olds." *Infant Behavior and Development* 50(2): 12–21.

Biringen, Zeynep, et al. 2012. "Emotional Availability, Attachment, and Intervention in Center-Based Child Care for Infants and Toddlers." *Development and Psychopathology* 24(1): 23–34.

Bocknek, Erika, et al. 2012. "Maternal Psychological Absence and Toddlers' Social-Emotional Development: Interpretations from the Perspective of Boundary Ambiguity Theory." *Family Process* 51(4): 527–541.

Botto, Sara Valencia, and Philippe Rochat. 2018. "Sensitivity to the Evaluation of Others Emerges by 24 Months." *Developmental Psychology* 54(9): 1723–1734.

Bowlby, John. 1969. *Attachment and Loss: Vol. 1: Attachment.* New York: Basic Books.

Braungart-Rieker, Julia, Ashley Hill-Soderlund, and Jan Karrass. 2010. "Fear and Anger Reactivity Trajectories from 4 to 16 Months: The Roles of Temperament, Regulation, and Maternal Sensitivity." *Developmental Psychology* 46(4): 791–804.

Briggs-Gowan, Margaret, and Alice Carter. 2008. "Social-Emotional Screening Status in Early Childhood Predicts Elementary School Outcomes." *Pediatrics* 121(5): 957–962.

Brock, Rebecca, and Grazyna Kochanska. 2019. "Anger in Infancy and Its Implications: History of Attachment in Mother-Child and Father-Child Relationships as a Moderator of Risk." *Development and Psychopathology* 31(4): 1353–1366.

Bronfenbrenner, Urie, ed. 2005. *Making Human Beings Human: Bioecological Perspectives on Human Development.* Thousand Oaks, CA: SAGE.

Brooker, Ivy, and Diane Poulin-Dubois. 2013. "Is a Bird an Apple? The Effect of Speaker Labeling Accuracy on Infants' Word Learning, Imitation, and Helping Behaviors." *Infancy* 18 (Suppl. 1): E46–E68.

Brooker, Rebecca, et al. 2014. "Profiles of Observed Infant Anger Predict Preschool Behavior Problems: Moderation by Life Stress." *Developmental Psychology* 50(10): 2343–2352.

Brophy-Herb, Holly, et al. 2015. "Toddlers with Early Behavioral Problems at Higher Family Demographic Risk Benefit the Most from Maternal Emotion Talk." *Journal of Development and Behavioral Pediatrics* 36(7): 512–520.

Brophy-Herb, Holly, et al. 2009. "Early Emotional Development in Infants and Toddlers: Perspectives of Early Head Start Staff and Parents." *Infant Mental Health Journal* 30(3): 203–222.

Brophy-Herb, Holly, et al. 2011. "Toddlers' Social-Emotional Competence in the Contexts of Maternal Emotion Socialization and Contingent Responsiveness in a Low-Income Sample." *Social Development* 20(1): 73–92.

Brownell, Celia A., et al. 2013. "Socialization of Early Prosocial Behavior: Parents' Talk about Emotions Is Associated with Sharing and Helping in Toddlers." *Infancy* 18(1): 91–119.

Burkhart, Margaret L., Jessica Borelli, Hannah Rasmussen, and David Sbarra. 2015. "Cherish the Good Times: Relational Savoring in Parents of Infants and Toddlers." *Personal Relationships* 22(4): 692–711.

Buss, Kristin A., and Elizabeth Kiel. 2004. "Comparison of Sadness, Anger, and Fear Facial Expressions When Toddlers Look at Their Mothers." *Child Development* 75(6): 1761–1773.

Buss, Kristin A., and Elizabeth Kiel. 2011. "Do Maternal Protective Behaviors Alleviate Toddlers' Fearful Distress?" *International Journal of Behavior Development* 35(2): 136–143.

Carlson, Frances M. 2006. *Essential Touch: Meeting the Needs of Young Children*. Washington, DC: NAEYC.

Campos, Belinda, et al. 2015. "Attuned to the Positive? Awareness and Responsiveness to Others' Positive Emotion Experience and Display." *Motivation and Emotion* 39(5): 780–794.

Castellanos, Irina, Melissa Shuman, and Lorraine Bahrick. 2004. "Intersensory Redundancy Facilitates Infants' Perception of Meaning in Speech Passages." Paper presented at the International Conference on Infant Studies, Chicago, IL, May.

Center for Early Childhood Mental Health Consultation. 2008. Types of Traumatic Experiences. https://www.ecmhc.org/tutorials/trauma/mod1_3.html

Center on the Developing Child. 2013. "InBrief: The Science of Neglect." https://developingchild.harvard.edu/resources/inbrief-the-science-of-neglect-video/

Center on the Developing Child. 2020a. A Guide to Serve and Return: How Your Interaction with Children Can Build Brains. https://developingchild.harvard.edu/guide/a-guide-to-serve-and-return-how-your-interaction-with-children-can-build-brains/

Center on the Developing Child. 2020b. "The Impact of Early Adversity on Children's Development." https://developingchild.harvard.edu/resources/inbrief-the-impact-of-early-adversity-on-childrens-development-video/

Center on the Developing Child. 2020c. Toxic Stress. https://developingchild.harvard.edu/science/key-concepts/toxic-stress/

Centers for Disease Control and Prevention. 2018. CDC's Developmental Milestones. https://www.cdc.gov/ncbddd/actearly/milestones/index.html

Centers for Disease Control and Prevention. n.d. *Milestone Moments: Learn the Signs. Act Early.* https://www.cdc.gov/ncbddd/actearly/pdf/booklets/Milestone-Moments-Booklet_Reader_508.pdf

Chen, Xinyin. 2018. "Culture, Temperament, and Social and Psychological Adjustment." *Developmental Review* 50: 42–53.

Chiarella, Sabrina, and Diane Poulin-Dubois. 2013. "Cry Babies and Pollyannas: Infants Can Detect Unjustified Emotional Reactions." *Infancy* 18(s1): E81–E96.

Chóliz, Mariano, Enrique Fernández-Abascal, and Francisco Martínez-Sánchez. 2012. "Infant Crying: Pattern of Weeping, Recognition of Emotion and Affective Reactions in Observers." *The Spanish Journal of Psychology* 15(3): 978–988.

Colorado Office of Early Childhood. 2019. Expanding Quality in Infant and Toddler Care Initiative. http://coloradoofficeofearlychildhood.force.com/oec/OEC_Providers?p=Providersands=Expanding-Quality-in-Infant-Toddler-Care-Initiativeandlang=en

Corbeil, Marieve, Sandra Trehub, and Isabelle Peretz. 2013. "Speech vs. Singing: Infants Choose Happier Sounds." *Frontiers in Psychology* 4: 372.

Cowen, Alan S., and Dacher Keltner. 2017. "Self-Report Captures 27 Distinct Categories of Emotion Bridged by Continuous Gradients." *Proceedings of the National Academy of Sciences of the United States of America* 114(38): E7900–E7909.

Crandall, Alice A., et al. 2018. "The Interface of Maternal Cognitions and Executive Function in Parenting and Child Conduct Problems." *Family Relations* 67(3): 339–353.

Dalli, Carmen. 2016. "Tensions and Challenges in Professional Practice with Under-Threes: A New Zealand Reflection on Early Childhood Professionalism as a Systemic Phenomenon." In *Under-Three-Year-Olds in Policy and Practice*. Singapore: Springer.

Davies, Ffion C., et al. 2015. "A Profile of Suspected Child Abuse as a Subgroup of Major Trauma Patients." *Emergency Medicine Journal* 32(12): 921–925.

Davis, Belinda, and Rosemary Dunn. 2018. "Making the Personal Visible: Emotion in the Nursery." *Early Child Development and Care* 188(7): 905–923.

Denham, Susanne A., et al. 2015. "'I Know How You Feel': Preschoolers' Emotion Knowledge Contributes to Early School Success." *Journal of Early Childhood Research* 13(3): 252–262.

Denham, Susanne A., Hideko Bassett, and Katherine Zinsser. 2012. "Early Childhood Teachers as Socializers of Young Children's Emotional Competence." *Early Childhood Education Journal* 40(3): 137–143.

Denham, Susanne A., et al. 2003. "Preschool Emotional Competence: Pathway to Social Competence?" *Child Development* 74(1): 238–256.

Denham, Susanne A., et al. 2016. "Key Considerations in Assessing Young Children's Emotional Competence." *Cambridge Journal of Education* 46(3): 399–317.

Djambazova-Popordanoska, Snezhana. 2016. "Implications of Emotion Regulation on Young Children's Emotional Well-Being and Educational Achievement." *Educational Review* 68(4): 497–515.

Dollar, Jessica M., and Kristin A. Buss. 2014. "Approach and Positive Affect in Toddlerhood Predict Early Childhood Behavior Problems." *Social Development* 23(2): 267–287.

Dollar, Jessica M., Cynthia Stifter, and Kristin A. Buss. 2017. "Exuberant and Inhibited Children: Person-Centered Profiles and Links to Social Adjustment." *Developmental Psychology* 53(7): 1222–1229.

Drummond, Jesse D. K., et al. 2017. "Helping the One You Hurt: Toddlers' Rudimentary Guilt, Shame, and Prosocial Behavior after Harming Another." *Child Development* 88(4): 1382–1397.

Duke University, Sanford School of Public Policy, Center for Child and Family Policy. 2020. Building Capacity for Trauma-Informed Infant and Toddler Care. https://childandfamilypolicy.duke.edu/project/building-capacity-for-trauma-informed-infant-toddler-care/

Ekman, Paul. 1999. "Basic Emotions." In *Handbook of Cognition and Emotion*. New York: John Wiley and Sons.

Elfer, Peter, and Jools Page. 2015. "Pedagogy with Babies: Perspectives of Eight Nursery Managers." *Early Child Development and Care* 185(11–12): 1762–1782.

Engle, Jennifer M., and Nancy McElwain. 2011. "Parental Reactions to Toddlers' Negative Emotions and Child Negative Emotionality as Correlates of Problem Behavior at the Age of Three." *Social Development* 20(2): 251–271.

Ensor, Rosie, and Claire Hughes. 2005. "More than Talk: Relations between Emotion Understanding and Positive Behaviour in Toddlers." *British Journal of Developmental Psychology* 23(3): 343–363.

Esposito, Gianluca, et al. 2013. "Infant Calming Responses During Maternal Carrying in Humans and Mice." *Current Biology* 23(9): 739–745.

Esseily, Rana, et al. 2015. "Humour Production May Enhance Observational Learning of a New Tool-Use Action in 18-Month-Old Infants." *Cognition and Emotion* 30(4): 817–825.

Fernández-Sánchez, Marta, Marta Giménez-Dasí, and Laura Quintanilla. 2014. "Toddlers' Understanding of Basic Emotions: Identification, Labeling and Causality/La comprensión temprana de las emociones básicas: Identificación, etiquetado y causalidad." *Infancia y Aprendizaje* 37(3): 569–601.

Ford, Brett Q., and Iris B. Mauss. 2015. "Culture and Emotion Regulation." *Current Opinion in Psychology* 3: 1–5.

Garner, Amanda. 2010. "Can a Mother's Affection Prevent Anxiety in Adulthood?" Health.com. https://www.health.com/condition/pregnancy/maternal-affection-anxiety

Gerhardt, Sue. 2015. *Why Love Matters: How Affection Shapes a Baby's Brain*. 2nd ed. New York: Routledge.

Giménez-Dasí, Marta, Marta Fernández-Sánchez, and Laura Quintanilla. 2015. "Improving Social Competence through Emotion Knowledge in 2-Year-Old Children: A Pilot Study." *Early Education and Development* 26(8): 1128–1144.

Goldstein, Thalia R., and Matthew D. Lerner. 2018. "Dramatic Pretend Play Games Uniquely Improve Emotional Control in Young Children." *Developmental Science* 21(4): e12603.

Grady, Jessica S., and Delaney Callan. 2019. "Shy Toddlers Act Bold: The Roles of Respiratory Sinus Arrhythmia and Parent Emotion Language." *Infant Behavior and Development* 55: 32–37.

Graham, Alice M., et al. 2015. "Early Life Stress Is Associated with Default System Integrity and Emotionality During Infancy." *Journal of Child Psychology and Psychiatry* 56(11): 1212–1222.

Grazzani, Ilaria, Veronica Ornaghi, Alessia Agliati, and Elisa Brazzelli. 2016. "How to Foster Toddlers' Mental-State Talk, Emotion Understanding, and Prosocial Behavior: A Conversation-Based Intervention at Nursery School." *Infancy* 21(2): 199–227.

Groeneveld, Marleen G., H. J. Vermeer, Marinus van IJzendoorn, and Mariëlle Linting. 2012. "Stress, Cortisol and Well-Being of Caregivers and Children in Home-Based Child Care: A Case for Differential Susceptibility." *Child Care Health and Development* 38(2): 251–260.

Groh, Ashley M., et al. 2017. "Mothers' Physiological and Affective Responding to Infant Distress: Unique Antecedents of Avoidant and Resistant Attachments." *Child Development* 90(2): 489–505.

Grossmann, Tobias, Manuela Missana, and Kathleen Krol. 2018. "The Neurodevelopmental Precursors of Altruistic Behavior in Infancy." *PLoS Biology* 16(9): e2005281.

Guedeney, Antoine, et al. 2014. "Social Withdrawal at 1 Year Is Associated with Emotional and Behavioural Problems at 3 and 5 Years: The Eden Mother-Child Cohort Study." *European Child and Adolescent Psychiatry* 23(12): 1181–1188.

Hall, Karyn. 2014. "Create a Sense of Belonging: Finding Ways to Belong Can Help Ease the Pain of Loneliness." *Psychology Today.* https://www.psychologytoday.com/us/blog/pieces-mind/201403/create-sense-belonging

Hanson, Jamie L., et al. 2015. "Family Poverty Affects the Rate of Human Infant Brain Growth." *PLoS ONE* 10(12): e0146434.

Harari, Yuval Noah. 2018. *21 Lessons for the 21st Century.* New York: Penguin Random House.

Havighurst, Sophie S., et al. 2019. "Tuning in to Toddlers: Research Protocol and Recruitment for Evaluation of an Emotion Socialization Program for Parents of Toddlers." *Frontiers in Psychology* 10: 1054.

Hay, Dale F., et al. 2014. "Precursors to Aggression Are Evident by 6 Months of Age." *Developmental Science* 17(3): 471–480.

Heck, Alison, et al. 2018. "Development of Body Emotion Perception in Infancy: From Discrimination to Recognition." *Infant Behavior and Development* 50: 42–51.

Hoehl, Stefanie, Lisa Wiese, and Tricia Striano. 2008. "Young Infants' Neural Processing of Objects Is Affected by Eye Gaze Direction and Emotional Expression." *PLoSONE* 3(6): e2389.

Hong, Yoo-Rha, and Jae Sun Park. 2012. "Impact of Attachment, Temperament, and Parenting on Human Development." *Korean Journal of Pediatrics* 55(12): 449–454.

Honig, Alice S. 2014. *The Best for Babies: Expert Advice for Assessing Infant-Toddler Programs.* Lewisville, NC: Gryphon House.

Honig, Alice S., and Donna S. Wittmer. 1985. "Toddler Bids and Teacher Responses." *Child Care Quarterly* 14(1): 14–30.

Hsiao, Celia, Nina Koren-Karie, Heidi Bailey, and Greg Moran. 2015. "It Takes Two to Talk: Longitudinal Associations among Infant-Mother Attachment, Maternal Attachment Representations, and Mother-Child Emotion Dialogues." *Attachment and Human Development* 17(1): 43–64.

Hunnius, Sabine, Tessa de Wit, Sven Vrins, and Claes von Hofsten. 2011. "Facing Threat: Infants' and Adults' Visual Scanning of Faces with Neutral, Happy, Sad, Angry, and Fearful Emotional Expressions." *Cognition and Emotion* 25(2): 193–205.

Hutt, Rachel L., Kristin A. Buss, and Elizabeth J. Kiel. 2013. "Caregiver Protective Behavior, Toddler Fear and Sadness, and Toddler Cortisol Reactivity in Novel Contexts." *Infancy* 18(5): 708–728.

Imrisek, Steven D., Katerina Castaño, and Kristin Bernard. 2018. "Developing Self-Regulation in a Dysregulating World: Attachment and Biobehavioral Catch-Up for a Toddler in Foster Care." *Journal of Clinical Psychology* 74(8): 1308–1318.

Izard, Carroll E. 1971. *The Face of Emotion*. New York: Appleton-Century-Crofts.

Izard, Carroll E. 1977. *Human Emotions*. New York: Plenum.

Jaekel, Julia, Suna Eryigit-Madzwamuse, and Dieter Wolke. 2015. "Preterm Toddlers' Inhibitory Control Abilities Predict Attention Regulation and Academic Achievement at Age 8 Years." *The Journal of Pediatrics* 169: 87–92.

Johnson, Heather, Laura Wilhelm, and Ginger Welch. 2013. *The Neglected Child: How to Recognize, Respond, and Prevent*. Lewisville, NC: Gryphon House.

Kaplan, Louise. 1998. *Oneness and Separateness: From Infant to Individual*. New York: Simon and Schuster.

Keltner, Dacher, and Daniel Cordaro. 2017. "Understanding Multimodal Emotional Expressions: Recent Advances in Basic Emotion Theory." In *The Science of Facial Expression*. New York: Oxford University Press.

Kiel, Elizabeth, Julie Premo, and Kristin Buss. 2016. "Maternal Encouragement to Approach Novelty: A Curvilinear Relation to Change in Anxiety for Inhibited Toddlers." *Journal of Abnormal Child Psychology* 44(3): 433–444.

King, Elizabeth K. 2020. "Fostering Toddlers' Social Emotional Competence: Considerations of Teachers' Emotion Language by Child Gender." *Early Child Development and Care* 1–14. 10.1080/03004430.2020.1718670.

King, Elizabeth K., and Karen La Paro. 2018. "Teachers' Emotion Minimizing Language and Toddlers' Social Emotional Competence." *Early Education and Development* 29(8): 989–1003.

Kistin, Caroline J., et al. 2014. "A Qualitative Study of Parenting Stress, Coping, and Discipline Approaches among Low-Income Traumatized Mothers." *Journal of Developmental and Behavioral Pediatrics* 35(3): 189–196.

Kobiella, Andrea, Tobias Grossmann, Vincent Reid, and Tricia Striano. 2008. "The Discrimination of Angry and Fearful Facial Expressions in 7-Month-Old Infants: An Event-Related Potential Study." *Cognition and Emotion* 22(1): 134–146.

Kok, Rianne, et al. 2015. "Normal Variation in Early Parental Sensitivity Predicts Child Structural Brain Development." *Journal of the American Academy of Child and Adolescent Psychiatry* 54(10): 824–831.

Konishi, Haruka, Ashley Karsten, and Claire Vallotton. 2018. "Toddlers' Use of Gesture and Speech in Service of Emotion Regulation During Distressing Routines." *Infant Mental Health Journal* 39(6): 730–750.

Krassner, Ariye M., et al. 2017. "East-West, Collectivist-Individualist: A Cross-Cultural Examination of Temperament in Toddlers from Chile, Poland, South Korea, and the U.S." *European Journal of Developmental Psychology* 14(4): 449–464.

Krøjgaard, Peter. 2005. "Infants' Search for Hidden Persons." *International Journal of Behavioral Development* 29(1): 70–79.

Kyzar, Kathleen B., Ann Turnbull, Jean Ann Summers, Viviana Aya Gómez. 2012. "The Relationship of Family Support to Family Outcomes: A Synthesis of Key Findings from Research on Severe Disability." *Research and Practice for Persons with Severe Disabilities* 37(1): 31–44.

Lally, J. Ronald, and Peter Mangione. 2017. "Caring Relationships: The Heart of Early Brain Development." *Young Children* 72(2): 17–24.

Lauw, Michelle S. M., et al. 2014. "Improving Parenting of Toddlers' Emotions Using an Emotion Coaching Parenting Program: A Pilot Study of Tuning in to Toddlers." *Journal of Community Psychology* 42(2): 169–175.

LeCuyer, Elizabeth, and Gail M. Houck. 2006. "Maternal Limit-Setting in Toddlerhood: Socialization Strategies for the Development of Self-Regulation." *Infant Mental Health Journal* 27(4): 344–370.

LeDoux, Joseph E., and Richard Brown. 2017. "A Higher-Order Theory of Emotional Consciousness." *Proceedings of the National Academy of Sciences of the United States of America* 114(10): E2016–E2015.

Lee, Vivian, Mariam Besada, and M. D. Rutherford. 2018. "Individual Differences in Emotional Expression Discrimination Are Associated with Emotion Label Production in Toddlers." *European Journal of Developmental Psychology* 15(5): 506–516.

Leventon, Jacqueline S., and Patricia J. Bauer. 2013. "The Sustained Effect of Emotional Signals on Neural Processing in 12-Month-Olds." *Developmental Science* 16(4): 485–498.

Lieberman, Alicia F. 2018. *The Emotional Life of the Toddler.* New York: Simon and Schuster.

Lindsey, Eric W., Penny Cremeens, Malinda Colwell, and Yvonne Caldera. 2009. "The Structure of Parent-Child Dyadic Synchrony in Toddlerhood and Children's Communication Competence and Self-Control." *Social Development* 18(2): 375–396.

Lisonbee, Jared A., Jacquelyn Mize, Amie Lapp Payne, and Douglas A. Granger. 2008. "Children's Cortisol and the Quality of Teacher-Child Relationships in Child Care." *Child Development* 79(6): 1818–1832.

LoBue, Vanessa. 2016. "Face Time: Here's How Infants Learn from Facial Expressions." The Conversation. https://theconversation.com/face-time-heres-how-infants-learn-from-facial-expressions-53327

Lomas, Tim. 2018. "The Quiet Virtues of Sadness: A Selective Theoretical and Interpretative Appreciation of Its Potential Contribution to Well-Being." *New Ideas in Psychology* 49: 18–26.

Luby, Joan L. 2015. "Poverty's Most Insidious Damage: The Developing Brain." *JAMA Pediatrics* 169(9): 810–811.

Lucca, Kelsey, Rachel Horton, and Jessica Sommerville. 2020. "Infants Rationally Decide When and How to Employ Effort." *Nature Human Behaviour.* https://doi.org/10.1038/s41562-019-0814-0

Mahler, Margaret, Fred Pine, and Anni Bergman. 1973. *The Psychological Birth of the Human Infant: Symbiosis and Individuation*. New York: Basic Books.

Mäntymaa Mirjami, et al. 2015. "Shared Pleasure in Early Mother-Infant Interaction: Predicting Lower Levels of Emotional and Behavioral Problems in the Child and Protecting against the Influence of Parental Psychopathology." *Infant Mental Health Journal* 36(2): 223–237.

Maselko, Joanna, Laura Kubzansky, Lewis Lipsitt, and Stephen Buka. 2011. "Mother's Affection at 8 Months Predicts Emotional Distress in Adulthood." *Journal of Epidemiology Community Health* 65(7): 621–625.

McAloon, John, and Karina Lazarou. 2019. "Preventative Intervention for Social, Emotional, and Behavioural Difficulties in Toddlers and Their Families: A Pilot Study." *International Journal of Environmental Research and Public Health* 16(4): E569.

Mcquaid, Nancy E., Maximilian Bibok, and Jeremy Carpendale. 2009. "Relation Between Maternal Contingent Responsiveness and Infant Social Expectations." *Infancy* 14(3): 390–401.

Meins, Elizabeth. 2013. "Sensitive Attunement to Infants' Internal States: Operationalizing the Construct of Mind-Mindedness." *Attachment and Human Development* 15(5): 524–544.

Meins, Elizabeth, Luna Centifanti, Charles Fernyhough, and Sarah Fishburn. 2013. "Maternal Mind-Mindedness and Children's Behavioral Difficulties: Mitigating the Impact of Low Socioeconomic Status." *Journal of Abnormal Child Psychology* 41(4): 543–553.

Meltzoff, Andrew N. 1985. "Immediate and Deferred Imitation in Fourteen- and Twenty-Four-Month-Old Infants." *Child Development* 56(1): 62–72.

Meltzoff, Andrew N. 2011. "Social Cognition and the Origins of Imitation, Empathy, and Theory Of Mind." In *The Wiley-Blackwell Handboook of Childhood Cognitive Development*. 2nd ed. Malden, MA: Wiley-Blackwell.

Michigan State University. 2015. "Helping Toddlers Understand Emotion Key to Development." ScienceDaily. https://www.sciencedaily.com/releases/2015/09/150901113445.htm

Mirabile, Scott, Laura Scaramella, Sara Sohr-Preston, and Sarah Robison. 2009. "Mothers' Socialization of Emotion Regulation: The Moderating Role of Children's Negative Emotional Reactivity." *Child and Youth Care Forum* 38(1): 19–37.

Mireault, Gina C. 2017. "Laughing Matters—And Helps to Explain How Babies Bond." *Scientific American Mind* 28(3): 44.

Mireault, Gina C., et al. 2018. "Social, Cognitive, and Physiological Aspects of Humour Perception from 4 to 8 Months: Two Longitudinal Studies." *British Journal of Developmental Psychology* 36(1): 98–109.

Mireault, Gina C., et al. 2014. "Social Looking, Social Referencing, and Humor Perception in 6-and 12-Month-Old Infants." *Infant Behavior and Development* 37(4): 536–545.

Morgan, Paul, et al. 2015. "24-Month-Old Children with Larger Oral Vocabularies Display Greater Academic and Behavioral Functioning at Kindergarten Entry." *Child Development* 86(5): 1351–1370.

Morris, Amanda S., Michael M. Criss, Jennifer S. Silk, and Benjamin J. Houltberg. 2017. "The Impact of Parenting on Emotion Regulation During Childhood and Adolescence." *Child Development Perspectives* 11(4): 233–238.

Mortensen, Jennifer A., and Melissa Barnett. 2015. "Teacher-Child Interactions in Infant/Toddler Child Care and Socioemotional Development." *Early Education and Development* 26(2): 209–229.

Mortensen, Jennifer A., and Melissa Barnett. 2016. "The Role of Child Care in Supporting the Emotion Regulatory Needs of Maltreated Infants and Toddlers." *Children and Youth Services Review* 64: 73–81.

Mortensen, Jennifer A., and Melissa Barnett. 2019. "Intrusive Parenting, Teacher Sensitivity, and Negative Emotionality on the Development of Emotion Regulation in Early Head Start." *Infant Behavior and Development* 55: 10–21.

Murray, Jane, and Ioanna Palaiologou. 2018. "Young Children's Emotional Experiences." *Early Child Development and Care* 188(7): 875–878.

Muzard, Antonia, et al. 2017. "Infants' Emotional Expression: Differences in the Expression of Pleasure and Discomfort between Infants from Chile and the United States." *Infant and Child Development* 26(6): e2033.

Narvaez, Darcia, and David Witherington. 2018. "Getting to Baselines for Human Nature, Development, and Well-Being." *Archives of Scientific Psychology* 6(1): 205–213.

National Association for the Education of Young Children. 2018. *Professional Standards and Competencies for Early Childhood Educators.* Draft. https://www.naeyc.org/sites/default/files/globally-shared/downloads/PDFs/resources/position-statements/public_draft_1.pdf

National Scientific Council on the Developing Child. 2004. *Children's Emotional Development Is Built into the Architecture of Their Brains: Working Paper No. 2.* https://46y5eh11fhgw3ve3ytpwxt9r-wpengine.netdna-ssl. com/wp-content/uploads/2004/04/Childrens-Emotional-Development-Is-Built-into-the-Architecture-of-Their-Brains.pdf

North Carolina Foundations Task Force. 2013. *North Carolina Foundations for Early Learning and Development.* Raleigh, NC: North Carolina Foundations Task Force. https://ncchildcare.ncdhhs.gov/Portals/0/documents/pdf/N/NC_Foundations.pdf

Noten, Malou, et al. 2019. "Empathic Distress and Concern Predict Aggression in Toddlerhood: The Moderating Role of Sex." *Infant Behavior and Development* 54: 57–65.

Nummenmaa, Lauri, Enrico Glerean, Riitta Hari, and Jari Hietanen. 2014. "Bodily Maps of Emotions." *Proceedings of the National Academy of Sciences of the United States of America* 111(2): 646–651.

Ornaghi, Veronica, Alessandro Pepe, Alessia Agliati, and Ilaria Grazzani. 2019. "The Contribution of Emotion Knowledge, Language Ability, and Maternal Emotion Socialization Style to Explaining Toddlers' Emotion Regulation." *Social Development* 28(3): 581–598.

Page, Jools. 2016. "Educators' Perspectives on Attachment and Professional Love in Early Years Settings in England." In *Under-Three Year Olds in Policy and Practice.* Singapore: Springer.

Piazza, Elise, Liat Hasenfratz, Uri Hasson, and Casey Lew-Williams. 2020. "Infant and Adult Brains Are Coupled to the Dynamics of Natural Communication." *Psychological Science* 31(1): 6-17.

Peltola, Mikko J., et al. 2015. "Attention to Faces Expressing Negative Emotion at 7 Months Predicts Attachment Security at 14 Months." *Child Development* 86(5): 1321–1332.

Plutchik, Robert. 2002. *Emotions and Life: Perspectives from Psychology, Biology, and Evolution.* Washington, DC: American Psychological Association.

Raval, Vaishali V., and Bethany Walker. 2019. "Unpacking 'Culture': Caregiver Socialization of Emotion and Child Functioning in Diverse Families." *Developmental Review* 51: 146–174.

Ravindran, Niyantri, Nancy McElwain, Daniel Berry, and Laurie Kramer. 2017. "Mothers' Dispositional Distress Reactivity as a Predictor of Maternal Support Following Momentary Fluctuations in Children's Aversive Behavior." *Developmental Psychology* 54(2): 209–219.

Razza, Rachel, Anne Martin, and Jeanne Brooks-Gunn. 2012. "Anger and Children's Socioemotional Development: Can Parenting Elicit a Positive Side to a Negative Emotion?" *Journal of Child and Family Studies* 21(5): 845–856.

Repacholi, Betty M., and Andrew Meltzoff. 2007. "Emotional Eavesdropping: Infants Selectively Respond to Indirect Emotional Signals." *Child Development* 78(2): 503–521.

Repacholi, Betty M., Andrew Meltzoff, and Berit Olsen. 2008. "Infants' Understanding of the Link between Visual Perception and Emotion: 'If She Can't See Me Doing It, She Won't Get Angry.'" *Developmental Psychology* 44(2): 561–574.

Repacholi, Betty M., Andrew Meltzoff, Theresa Hennings, and Ashley Ruba. 2016. "Transfer of Social Learning Across Contexts: Exploring Infants' Attribution of Trait-Like Emotions to Adults." *Infancy* 21(6): 785–806.

Repacholi, Betty M., Andrew Meltzoff, Hillary Rowe, and Tamara Toub. 2014. "Infant, Control Thyself: Infants' Integration of Multiple Social Cues to Regulate Their Imitative Behavior." *Cognitive Development* 32: 46–57.

Riem, Madelon, and Annemiek Karreman. 2019. "Experimental Manipulation of Emotion Regulation Changes Mothers' Physiological and Facial Expressive Responses to Infant Crying." *Infant Behavior and Development* 55: 22–31.

Roben, Caroline, Pamela Cole, and Laura Marie Armstrong. 2013. "Longitudinal Relations among Language Skills, Anger Expression, and Regulatory Strategies in Early Childhood." *Child Development* 84(3): 891–905.

Rubin, Kenneth H., Kim Burgess, and Paul Hastings. 2002. "Stability and Social-Behavioral Consequences of Toddlers' Inhibited Temperament and Parenting Behaviors." *Child Development* 73(2): 483–495.

Salamon, Andi, Jennifer Sumsion, and Linda Harrison. 2017. "Infants Draw on 'Emotional Capital' in Early Childhood Education Contexts: A New Paradigm." *Contemporary Issues in Early Childhood* 18(4): 362–374.

Salzwedel, Andrew P., et al. 2018. "Development of Amygdala Functional Connectivity during Infancy and Its Relationship with 4-Year Behavioral Outcomes." *Biological Psychiatry: Cognitive Neuroscience and Neuroimaging* 4(1): 62–71.

Santamaria, Lorena, et al. 2019. "Emotional Valence Modulates the Topology of the Parent-Infant Inter-Brain Network." *Neuroimage* 207. https://doi.org/10.1016/j.neuroimage.2019.116341

Saunders, Hannah, Allyson Kraus, Lavinia Barone, and Zeynep Biringen. 2015. "Emotional Availability: Theory, Research, and Intervention." *Frontiers in Psychology* 6: 1069.

Schoppmann, Johanna, Silvia Schneider, and Sabine Seehagen. 2019. "Wait and See: Observational Learning of Distraction as an Emotion Regulation Strategy in 22-Month-Old Toddlers." *Journal of Abnormal Child Psychology* 47(5): 851–863.

Sciaraffa, Mary A., Paula Zeanah, and Charles Zeanah. 2018. "Understanding and Promoting Resilience in the Context of Adverse Childhood Experiences." *Early Childhood Education Journal* 46(3): 343–353.

Senehi, Neda, Holly Brophy-Herb, and Claire Vallotton. 2018. "Effects of Maternal Mentalization-Related Parenting on Toddlers' Self-Regulation." *Early Childhood Research Quarterly* 44: 1–14.

Sethna, Vaheshta, et al. 2017. "Mother-Infant Interactions and Regional Brain Volumes in Infancy: An MRI Study." *Brain Structure and Function* 222: 2379–2388.

Shai, Dana, and Jay Belsky. 2017. "Parental Embodied Mentalizing: How the Nonverbal Dance between Parents and Infants Predicts Children's Socio-Emotional Functioning." *Attachment and Human Development* 19(2): 191–219.

Shai, Dana, Daphna Dollberg, and Ohad Szepsenwol. 2017. "The Importance of Parental Verbal and Embodied Mentalizing in Shaping Parental Experiences of Stress and Coparenting." *Infant Behavior and Development* 49: 87–96.

Shai, Dana, and Elizabeth Meins. 2018. "Parental Embodied Mentalizing and Its Relation to Mind-Mindedness, Sensitivity, and Attachment Security." *Infancy* 23(6): 857–872.

Skerry, Amy E., and Elizabeth Spelke. 2014. "Preverbal Infants Identify Emotional Reactions That Are Incongruent with Goal Outcomes." *Cognition* 130(2): 204–216.

Song, Ju-Hyun, et al. 2018. "Positive Parenting Moderates the Association between Temperament and Self-Regulation in Low-Income Toddlers." *Journal of Child and Family Studies* 27(7): 2354–2364.

Spinrad, Tracy L., and Diana Gal. 2018. "Fostering Prosocial Behavior and Empathy in Young Children." *Current Opinion in Psychology* 20: 4–44.

Sullivan, Margaret W., and Dennis Carmody. 2018. "Approach-Related Emotion, Toddlers' Persistence, and Negative Reactions to Failure." *Social Development* 27(3): 586–600.

Suor, Jennifer H., et al. 2015. "Tracing Differential Pathways of Risk: Associations among Family Diversity, Cortisol, and Cognitive Functioning in Childhood." *Child Development* 86(4): 1142–1158.

Svinth, Lone. 2018. "Being Touched: The Transformative Potential of Nurturing Touch Practices in Relation to Toddlers' Learning and Emotional Well-Being." *Early Child Development and Care* 188(7): 924–936.

Tremblay, Helene, Philippe Brun, and Jaqueline Nadel. 2005. "Emotion Sharing and Emotion Knowledge: Typical and Impaired Development." In *Emotional Development: Recent Research Advances*. Oxford, UK: Oxford University Press.

U.S. Department of Health and Human Services and U. S. Department of Education. 2017. *Social and Emotional Development Research Background*. https://www2.ed.gov/about/inits/ed/earlylearning/talk-read-sing/feelings-research.pdf

Vaillant-Molina, Mariana, Lorraine Bahrick, and Ross Flom. 2013. "Young Infants Match Facial and Vocal Emotional Expressions of Other Infants." *Infancy* 18(s1): E97–E111.

Vaish, Amrisha, Tobias Grossmann, and Amanda Woodward. 2008. "Not All Emotions Are Created Equal: The Negativity Bias in Social-Emotional Development." *Psychological Bulletin* 134(3): 383–403.

Vaish, Amrisha, and Tricia Striano. 2004. "Is Visual Reference Necessary? Contributions of Facial Versus Vocal Cues in 12-Month-Olds' Social Referencing Behavior." *Developmental Science* 7(3): 261–269.

Vallotton, Claire D. 2008. "Signs of Emotion: What Can Preverbal Children 'Say' About Internal States?" *Infant Mental Health Journal* 29(3): 234–258.

Vallotton, Claire D. 2009. "Do Infants Influence Their Quality of Care? Infants' Communicative Gestures Predict Caregivers' Responsiveness." *Infant Behavior and Development* 32(4): 351–365.

Walker, Gareth. 2017. "Young Children's Use of Laughter as a Means of Responding to Questions." *Journal of Pragmatics* 112: 20–32.

Warren, Susan L., Polina Umylny, Emily Aron, and Samuel Simmens. 2006. "Toddler Anxiety Disorders: A Pilot Study." *Journal of the American Academy of Child and Adolescent Psychiatry* 45(7): 859–866.

Weir, Kirsten. 2017. "Maximizing Children's Resilience." American Psychological Association. https://www.apa.org/monitor/2017/09/cover-resilience

Wijeakumar, Sobanawartiny, et al. 2019. "Early Adversity in Rural India Impacts the Brain Networks Underlying Visual Working Memory." *Developmental Science* 22(5): e12822.

Wilutzky, Wendy. 2015. "Emotions as Pragmatic and Epistemic Actions." *Frontiers in Psychology* 6: 1593.

Wittmer, Donna S. 2020. "The ABCDRs of Guidance with Infants and Toddlers." Unpublished paper. Microsoft Word file.

Wittmer, Donna S., and Deanna W. Clauson. 2018. *From Biting to Hugging: Understanding Social Development in Infants and Toddlers*. Lewisville, NC: Gryphon House.

Wittmer, Donna S., and Alice S. Honig. 2020. *Day to Day the Relationship Way: Creating Responsive Programs for Infants and Toddlers*. Washington, DC: NAEYC.

Wittmer, Donna S., and Sandy Petersen. 2018. *Infant and Toddler Development and Responsive Program Planning: A Relationship-Based Approach*. New York: Pearson.

Xiao, Sonya X., Tracy Spinrad, and D. Bruce Carter. 2018. "Parental Emotion Regulation and Preschoolers' Prosocial Behavior: The Mediating Roles of Parental Warmth and Inductive Discipline." *Journal of Genetic Psychology* 179(5): 246–255.

Yates, Tweety, et al. 2008. "Research Synthesis on Screening and Assessing Social-Emotional Competence." Nashville, TN: Center on the Social and Emotional Foundations for Early Learning, Vanderbilt University. http://csefel.vanderbilt.edu/documents/rs_screening_assessment.pdf

Zeegers, Moniek, Cristina Colonnesi, Geert Jan Stams, and Elizabeth Meins. 2017. "Mind Matters: A Meta-Analysis of Parental Mentalization and Sensitivity as Predictors of Infant-Parent Attachment." *Psychological Bulletin* 143(2): 1245–1272.

Zeng, Songtian, Xiaoyi Hu, Hongxia Zhao, and Angela K. Stone-MacDonald. 2020. "Examining the Relationships of Parental Stress, Family Support, and Family Quality of Life: A Structural Equation Modeling Approach." *Research in Developmental Disabilities* 96. 10.1016/j.ridd.2019.103523.

# Index

emotionally responsive environment, 80, 87, 95

emotionally responsive, 80, 85–86, 95

helping children feel a sense of belonging, 80, 82–83, 94

partnering with parents, 80, 92–93, 95

reading and singing about emotions, 80, 91–92, 95

responsive, 80, 84, 95

social-emotional activities for adults, 80, 94, 95

using emotional activities, 80, 88–90, 95

using routines, 80, 90–91, 95

## D

Deferred imitation, 67

Deliberate thinking, 118–119

Depression, 32, 51, 100–105, 109, 112–113, 122

Despair, 100–101, 105

Diapering, 90–91

Diminishing feelings, 6, 21, 70–71, 128

Discipline, positive and gentle, 50, 61–62

Distraction, 42–43

Distress, 50, 57–58, 112–113, 116, 123

Documentation, 44–47

Dolls, 89–90, 95, 116

Dramatic play, 84, 88–90, 116

## E

Early Learning and Development Guidelines (North Carolina), 46

Eating disturbances, 114

Embarrassment, 104–105

Emotion bridging, 66, 71–72

Emotion talk, 66, 71–72

Emotional activities, 80, 88–90, 95

Emotional brain, 26–28, 33

Emotional capital, 26–27, 33

Emotional coaching, 128

Emotional competence, vii, 4, 9–23, 26–33, 43–44, 49–63, 65–77

Emotional detection, 10–11, 14–15, 20–21, 27, 36–38, 40–41, 66–69

Emotional development, 126, 128

Emotional expression, 5, 11, 16, 20–21, 36, 38–39, 41, 47, 66, 69–70, 82–83

Emotional intelligence, 13, 20–21, 88

Emotional skills development, 35–47

Emotional socialization, 21–22

Emotional support, 121–122

Emotional understanding, 10–11, 13–15

Emotionally based story form, 86

Emotionally responsive curriculum, 80, 85–86, 95

Emotions, 2–7, 13, 21, 129

Empathy, 2, 5, 10–11, 14–15, 40, 50, 55, 67, 118

Environment, 80, 82–83, 87, 111, 113, 123

Expected behaviors, by age, 46

Experiences that support emotional competence, 29–31

Exposure to violence, 109, 114–115

Eye contact, 16–17, 30, 67, 74

## F

Facial expression, 2, 36–38, 66, 73–74, 91

Families

cultural diversity, 10, 21–23

discipline techniques, 119

encouraging to read, 80, 92–93, 95

needing intensive support, 121–122

partnering to understand children, 105

partnering with, vii, 21–23, 62, 76, 86, 111, 116, 126, 128, 131

Family violence, 109, 114–115

Fear, 31–32, 101–102, 105, 114, 120

Feeding, 90–91

Foster care, 114, 116

Frustration, 50, 57–58, 67–68, 103–105

Self-efficacy, 12, 18–19

Self-esteem, 29

Self-regulation, 10, 12, 17–18, 28, 47
    importance of, 29
    infants, 36, 40
    positive discipline and, 61–62
    teaching, 50, 56–57
    toddlers, 42–43
    toxic stress and, 113–114
    your own, 126, 129, 131

Sense of belonging, 80, 82–83, 94

Sensory challenges, 120

Separation anxiety, 101–102

"Serve and return" conversations, 84, 90-91, 94, 116

Shame, 41, 104–105

Shaming, 13, 70–71, 104, 114, 119

Sharing, 101

Shyness, 102, 105, 120

Sign language, 17, 40, 66, 71, 74–75

Singing, 80, 82, 86, 91–92, 95

Sleep disturbances, 114

Smiling, 38–39, 45, 101

Social referencing, 5, 37

Social skills, 28

Social-emotional activities for adults, 80, 94–96

Softness, 111

Stranger anxiety, 102

Stress, 31–32, 51
    emotional, 107–123
    positive and tolerable, 108–111, 122
    social stress, 108–109, 117–120, 123
    therapy or intervention, 108, 121–122
    toxic, 31–32, 108–109, 112–116, 122–123
    types of, 108–109
    what to do with your own, 130

Strong feelings
    responding to, 50, 57–58
    managing, 10, 17–19, 29, 36, 40, 42-43, 47, 50, 56-58

Supporting children's feelings, 97–103, 105
    anger and frustration, 103–105
    curiosity, confidence, and courage, 101, 105
    embarrassment, shame, and guilt, 104–105
    fear, worry, and anxiety, 101–102, 105
    happiness, joy, and glee, 99–100, 105
    love, affection, and security, 98–99, 105
    sadness, despair, depression, and grief, 100–101, 105

Supporting children's temperaments, 97, 104–105

T

Tantrums, 50, 57–58, 103, 112–113

Teacher-child interaction strategies, 65–77
    acknowledging feelings, 66, 70–71
    detecting emotions, 66–67
    developing emotional expression, 66, 69–70
    emotion talk and emotion bridging, 66, 71–72
    emphasizing causes of emotions, 66, 72–73
    facial expressions and tone of voice, 66, 73–74
    helping children read others' emotions, 66, 68–69
    managing your own emotions, 66, 75–76
    modeling emotions, 66–68
    teaching sign language, 66, 74–75

Threat, 37–38

Thumb sucking, 40, 42–43, 57

Toddlers
    active learners, 80, 83–84
    emotional activities, 88–90
    emotional skills development, 40–43
    expressing feelings, 41
    identifying feelings, 40–41
    managing emotions, 42–43
    reading to, 92
    understanding causes of feelings, 42

Tolerable stress, 108–111, 122
    Care for the Spirit Days, 110–111
    developing secure attachments, 110

Tone of voice, 66, 73–74, 116

Touch, 30, 50, 52–54